Richard Caplan

A New Trusteeship?

The International Administration of War-torn Territories

Adelphi Paper 341

Oxford University Press, Great Clarendon Street, Oxford OX2 6DP
Oxford   New York
Athens Auckland Bangkok Bombay Calcutta Cape Town
Dar es Salaam Delhi Florence Hong Kong Istanbul Karachi
Kuala Lumpur Madras Madrid Melbourne Mexico City
Nairobi Paris Singapore Taipei Tokyo Toronto
and associated companies in
Berlin Ibadan

Oxford is a trade mark of Oxford University Press

Published in the United States
by Oxford University Press Inc., New York

© The International Institute for Strategic Studies 2002

First published February 2002 by **Oxford University Press** for
The International Institute for Strategic Studies
Arundel House, 13–15 Arundel Street, Temple Place, London WC2R 3DX
www.iiss.org

Director John Chipman
Editor Mats R. Berdal
Assistant Editor John Wheelwright

British Library Cataloguing in Publication Data
Data available

Library of Congress Cataloguing in Publication Data

ISBN 0-19-851565-0
ISSN 0567-932x

Contents

Glossary

CIVPOL	Civilian Police
CNRT	National Council of Timorese Resistance
DPA	Department of Political Affairs
DPKO	Department of Peacekeeping Operations
DSRSG	Deputy Special Representative of the Secretary-General
ECOWAS	Economic Community of West African States
ETDF	East Timor Defence Force
ETTA	East Timor Transitional Administration
EU	European Union
FRETILIN	Revolutionary Front for the Independence of East Timor
FRY	Federal Republic of Yugoslavia (Serbia and Montenegro)
HR	High Representative
IAC	Interim Administrative Council
ICTY	International Criminal Tribunal for the former Yugoslavia
IFOR	Implementation Force
IMTF	Integrated Mission Task Force
INTERFET	International Force East Timor
IPTF	International Police Task Force
JIAS	Joint Interim Administrative Structure
KFOR	Kosovo Force
KLA	Kosovo Liberation Army
KPC	Kosovo Protection Corps

KTC	Kosovo Transitional Council
NC	National Council
NCC	National Consultative Council
OCHA	Office for the Co-ordination of Humanitarian Affairs
OHR	Office of the High Representative
OSCE	Organisation for Security and Co-operation in Europe
PDSRSG	Principal Deputy Special Representative of the Secretary-General
PIC	Peace Implementation Council
RRTF	Refugee Return Task Force
RS	Republika Srpska
SFOR	Stabilisation Force
SRSG	Special Representative of the Secretary-General
TA	Transitional Administrator
UNAMET	United Nations Assistance Mission in East Timor
UNHCR	United Nations High Commissioner for Refugees
UNMEE	United Nations Mission in Ethiopia and Eritrea
UNMIK	United Nations Interim Administration Mission in Kosovo
UNSAS	United Nations Standby Arrangements System
UNTAC	United Nations Transitional Authority in Cambodia
UNTAES	United Nations Transitional Administration for Eastern Slavonia, Baranja and Western Sirmium
UNTAET	United Nations Transitional Administration in East Timor
UNTAG	United Nations Transitional Assistance Group
UNTEA	United Nations Temporary Executive Authority

Introduction

Since the mid-1990s there has been a willingness to entrust the
United Nations and other multilateral bodies with more and more
authority for the administration of war-torn territories. In Bosnia,
Eastern Slavonia, Kosovo and East Timor these international organisations have assumed responsibility for governance to a degree unprecedented in recent history. Similar arrangements have
been proposed at various times for other zones of crisis or con-
tention, including Somalia, Sierra Leone, Kashmir, the city of
Jerusalem and, more recently, Afghanistan. An idea that once
enjoyed limited academic currency at best – international trusteeship for failed states and contested territories – has become a
reality in all but name.[1]

With the end of the Cold War, the vast majority of major
armed conflicts – averaging 28 a year – have been of an internal
nature, giving rise to brutal atrocities and rendering some states
incapable of performing even the most basic governmental functions.[2] At the same time, an increase in the importance that many
states attach to humanitarian norms as matters of international
concern, and a marked disregard for sovereignty as a barrier to
humanitarian interference, have facilitated the pursuit of policies of
a highly intrusive nature. Prompted in part by humanitarian considerations, the UN Security Council has authorised military interventions in Somalia, Rwanda, Haiti, Bosnia, Albania and East
Timor. Even 'unilateral' interventions of a humanitarian nature –
by the Nigerian-led ECOWAS in Liberia; France, Britain and the

United States in northern Iraq; and NATO in Yugoslavia – have attracted broad international support.[3] Some of these same intervening states, in turn, have perceived the need for international mechanisms to insure against the recurrence of fighting and, more ambitiously, to orchestrate the transition from conflict to peace. 'In the past we talked too much of exit strategies. But having made a commitment we cannot simply walk away once the fight is over,' Tony Blair, the British Prime Minister, declared in April 1999, during the NATO campaign against Yugoslavia (and two months before the establishment of the UN interim administration in Kosovo).[4]

In supporting the establishment of these transitional authorities, however, states have also been motivated by considerations of *Realpolitik*. Unable to insulate themselves from the effects of instability in the former Yugoslavia, the member states of the European Union have favoured a strong and extensive international presence in the region in the hope of establishing a lasting peace from which they, too, would benefit. Moreover, the EU's failure to offer an effective response to the crisis in the Balkans from its early days has led the Union to seek a leadership position in the post-war rule and reconstruction of these territories, partly to strengthen its own credibility in foreign policy-making. Similarly, Australia, concerned about instability and a possible refugee crisis originating off of its northern shore, was making preparations well before the outbreak of violence in East Timor to spearhead a military deployment there[5] and has taken a strong interest in the administration of the territory subsequently. Whether the more parochial interests of these states, which have provided some of the necessary impetus for international action, are entirely compatible with the broader purposes for which these initiatives have been conceived is one of the many issues that hang over these operations.

If international administration reflects a shift in international concerns, it is also consistent with another trend: the expansion of traditional peacekeeping operations to embrace a wide variety of 'peace-building' activities ranging from human-rights monitoring and electoral assistance to the protection of humanitarian relief operations and the disarmament, cantonment and demobilisation of armed forces. It would be a mistake, however, to suggest that international administration constitutes a mere extension of complex peacekeeping. The responsibilities that the United Nations and other international bodies have had to assume in these new operations are unique. Never before has a mission had to make and enforce local laws, exercise total fiscal management of a territory, appoint and remove public officials, create a central bank, establish and maintain customs services, regulate the local media, adjudicate rival property claims, run schools, regulate local businesses and reconstruct and operate all public utilities, among numerous other functions. In short, no international field operation has been vested with as much executive, legislative and judicial authority as some of the international administrations that have been established in the past six years.[6]

As the challenges are unique, so too are many of the questions these operations raise. Under what circumstances is it legitimate – and for whom – to administer distressed territories? How much authority should be entrusted to transitional administrators? To whom should international administrations be accountable? How are the aims of the international community and those of the local parties to be reconciled when they come into conflict? To what extent should transitional authorities seek to transform the societies over which they exercise authority, and towards what ends? When does 'benign' administration become neo-colonialism, and how is that to be avoided? By what criteria do we measure the success of a transitional administration? How should the transfer of power to the local population be regulated and the exit of the international authorities achieved?

With a view to addressing these questions, this paper examines recent experiences in the administration of war-torn territories. It identifies the different forms of international administration and explores the significance of the distinctions among them. It analyses and assesses the effectiveness of international transitional authorities and discusses, in thematic fashion, the key issues – strategic, political and economic – that arise in the context of these experiences. It also reflects on the policy implications of these experiences, recommending reforms or new approaches to international administration. The paper is concerned principally with operations in Eastern Slavonia, Bosnia, Kosovo and East Timor, but it draws on relevant antecedent experiences as well, including the International Control Commission for Albania (1913–14), the League of Nations administration of the Saarland (1920–35), the Allied occupation of Germany and Japan, the United Nations administration of trusteeship territories and various UN peace operations. Each situation is different: objective conditions vary; so, too, does the nature of the underlying problem. Kosovo is essentially a dispute over the control of territory whose future status is unclear, whereas the challenge in East Timor resembles that of a classical trusteeship on the eve of independence. In thinking about policy prescription, therefore, it would be wrong to assume that 'one size fits all'. Nonetheless, certain features common to all of these operations make it fruitful to view them from a global perspective.

Numerous factors contribute to the success or otherwise of an international administration. The central argument of this paper, however, is that a transitional administration in possession of full executive, as opposed to supervisory, authority is better equipped to meet the manifold challenges of these operations. While it may not always be necessary for administrators to exercise full authority (and they should seek to devolve as much responsibility to the local population as feasible), without such authority they are more likely to be obstructed by local actors in their efforts to achieve the aims of their mandates. The difficulty lies in determining where, in practice, to establish the balance between the competing demands of international responsibility, on the one hand, and local self-determination, on the other.

Any agency that has extensive authority must, of course, be carefully controlled to insure against abuse of power. That does not mean, however, that a transitional administration should strive to be a neutral party. A further argument of this paper is that international administration is fundamentally a political enterprise, and that, to succeed, a transitional authority cannot be indifferent to political outcomes. With respect to elections in Bosnia, for instance, it is not simply the process that matters (free and fair elections), but also the results (the marginalisation of militant nationalists and the strengthening of central government institutions). Similarly, in negotiating international treaties on behalf of

East Timor, the United Nations must be able to represent the interests of one party (East Timor) against the interests of others, including members of the United Nations. This is perhaps the most critical difference between international administration and complex peacekeeping. The United Nations and other international organisations have come to appreciate the need to navigate with the aid of a political compass, some preoccupations with impartiality notwithstanding. Yet what remains unclear is the *kind* of political engagement that is required. Where international authorities are highly interventionary, there is a risk of creating the administrative equivalent of donor dependency, in which the local population becomes accustomed to international representatives making decisions for them, including some of the harder decisions that they can thus choose to ignore. There is also the risk that political engagement may turn international administrators into merely another 'faction'. One of the principal challenges for transitional authorities, then, is to conceive a set of norms appropriate to the political tasks of international stewardship.

The geopolitical circumstances that have given rise to these operations may have been unique, and so one cannot know whether there will be the political will to establish more operations of this kind in the future. Indeed, despite the trends explored in this paper, there is a deep reluctance in the international community to become involved in the business of administering the territories of other states and other peoples, and – in the South in particular – there is concern that the development agenda may be sidetracked by such costly initiatives. There is also deep-seated anxiety in many countries about facilitating big-power interventions world-wide.[7] Still, internal conflicts persist, and further state fragmentation appears to be on the horizon. The United Nations and other multilateral agencies are likely to play some role in the administration of some of these territories, as in Afghanistan following the US-led military campaign there. The failure to reflect broadly on recent experiences and to draw what lessons one can from them will leave the international community ill-prepared for the tasks of administration in any future such missions that may be established.

Chapter 1

Forms of International Administration

The term 'international administration' embraces a wide range of experiences, historical and contemporary. In its present guise it is not a formal practice or institution in the way that UN trusteeship, or even UN peacekeeping, is. It has no specific UN Charter mandate, and there is no dedicated bureaucracy to support it, although all recent operations – UN or otherwise – have enjoyed the backing of the Security Council, and many UN departments and state ministries have committed full-time resources to the maintenance of these operations. International administration is an innovation, and an *ad hoc* one at that. In spite of this, one can talk about forms of international administration – operational categories, mandates and structures – in much the same way as one talks about these aspects of peace operations.

Operational Categories

One can usefully distinguish the various types of international administration on the basis of the degree of authority that the international community assumes in each case.[1] It is possible to imagine these different operations as lying along a continuum, with supervision at one end and direct governance at the other, the operations between the two exhibiting varying magnitudes of control.

The UN Transitional Authority in Cambodia (UNTAC) is a good example of international administration as supervision. UN-TAC was established in February 1992 to implement the Paris

Accords that sought to end the conflict among the four Cambodian factions.[2] As originally conceived – and in a striking departure from previous peacekeeping experiences – the United Nations was to exercise direct control over five critical areas of each faction's administrative structures (defence, foreign affairs, finance, information and public security) for a period of eighteen months, with the aim of establishing a 'neutral political environment conducive to free and fair general elections'.[3] (The UN had other tasks as well, but these were more consistent with expanded notions of peacekeeping.) In the event, the UN never did exert direct control. A host of problems – insufficient resources on the part of the UN; the Special Representative's preference for a consensual approach; intransigence by the incumbent Hun Sen government, in particular; and the difficulty of assuming governance functions for a limited period, especially in the administration of justice – forced the organisation to scale back its ambitions and accept a more modest role in supervising and monitoring the four factions' activities. Even in this more modest capacity, UNTAC at the time was the most extensive – and expensive – operation that the UN had ever launched.[4]

At the other end of the spectrum, international administration takes the form of direct governance, as exemplified by three operations: the UN Transitional Administration for Eastern Slavonia, Baranja and Western Sirmium (UNTAES), the UN Interim Administration Mission in Kosovo (UNMIK) and the UN Transitional Administration in East Timor (UNTAET). The first (and smallest) of these, UNTAES, was established in January 1996 for a period of twelve months, and then extended for another twelve months, to oversee the peaceful restoration to Croatia of the last remaining Serb-held region of this former Yugoslav republic.[5] It was only the second time in the UN's history that the organisation has been given a mandate to administer a disputed territory – the first had been in 1962–3, with the United Nations Temporary Executive Authority (UNTEA) in West New Guinea (West Irian).[6] The authority given to UNTAES was extensive: the Basic Agreement signed by the Croatian government and the local Serb leadership, which formed the basis of the enabling resolution, called upon the Security Council to establish an administration to 'govern' the region.[7] The Secretary-General's Special Representative in turn conceived a regime in which the 'transitional authority alone would have executive power and he would not have to obtain the consent of either the council or the parties for his decisions'.[8] In contrast to UNMIK and UNTAET, however, UNTAES did not perform many of the tasks of administration itself; it devolved considerable responsibility for administration of the territory to the local population, overriding their decisions when necessary.

Both UNMIK and UNTAET were established in 1999, following military conflicts that produced acute administrative vacuums in their wake. NATO's eleven-week bombing campaign against the Federal Republic of Yugoslavia (FRY), which aimed to weaken the Yugoslav forces engaged in the violent repression of Kosovo Albanians, precipitated a complete withdrawal of the FRY authorities from the province, leaving no functioning public administration at all.[9] The problem was compounded by the fact that vital institutions, such as health and education, had suffered from years of neglect and, more recently, the scorched-earth tactics of the departing Serbs.[10] Local insurgents, it was feared, would exploit the vacuum in an effort to seize political control, and the security of all people living in Kosovo – whether Serbs, Turks, Roma or Albanians – would be at risk. UN Security Council Resolution 1244 effectively established Kosovo as a UN protectorate, with NATO-led military forces providing an 'international security presence' and UNMIK performing all basic civil administrative functions.[11]

In East Timor, similarly, UNTAET has been given full responsibility for the administration of this former Indonesian-occupied territory. The mission was established in response to the crisis conditions that emerged there after the 'popular consultation' held on 30 August 1999, in which an overwhelming majority of East Timorese – 78.5 percent of the voting population – rejected autonomy within Indonesia and opted for independence. In reaction to the ballot results, the Indonesian armed forces and locally organised militia unleashed a devastating campaign of violence that left hundreds dead, displaced more than three-quarters of the population and destroyed some 70 percent of the territory's physical infrastructure.[12] On 15 September the UN Security Council authorised the deployment of an Australian-led multinational force

(INTERFET) to restore peace and security in East Timor and then, on 25 October, established UNTAET to administer the territory.[13] UNTAET effectively constitutes the legal sovereign in East Timor, and its authority arguably exceeds those of UNTAES and UNMIK in Eastern Slavonia and Kosovo.[14]

Between the poles of supervision and direct governance are operations that exhibit varying degrees of control over the territory in question. The international administration of Bosnia, which has no formal name, was established as part of a complex peace process that culminated in the 1995 signing of the General Framework Agreement for Peace in Bosnia and Herzegovina, better known as the Dayton Accord. The situation was unlike those in Kosovo and East Timor, but much like that in Cambodia: the three wartime regimes remained intact after the war, and the international community, in the embodiment of a High Representative, was empowered merely to 'monitor' implementation of the peace settlement and to 'promote' compliance with it, relying largely on the co-operation of the local parties to fulfil their obligations.[15] Over time, however, the High Representative has been given more authority, including the power to dismiss local officials deemed to be obstructing implementation of the accord and to issue interim laws if the local parties are 'unable' (that is, unwilling) to do so. Within the framework of the Office of the High Representative (OHR), a separate administration for the disputed area of Brčko was established in February 1997 under the authority of a 'Supervisor' enjoying more sweeping powers initially than the High Representative.[16]

In the first instance, then, what distinguishes these operations from one another is the degree of authority they possess. On the other hand, what distinguishes all of them from peacekeeping is the scope of their interest in, if not actual responsibility for, the functioning of a territory or state – extending in some cases to actual 'state-building'. Even UNTAC, limited though its mandate ultimately was, concerned itself with aspects of governance that lie outside the boundaries of peacekeeping, however conceived – from the elaboration of local administrative procedures and budget preparation to revenue collection, procurement and customs control. Thus, while the authority vested in these operations differs, they share a common preoccupation with governance of a comprehensive nature.

Operational Aims and Contextual Factors

If these operations can be distinguished from one another in terms of the authority they possess, they are further distinguished by their operational aims and the contextual factors or facts on the ground, which form what Pjer Šimunović calls the ' "outer ring" around the actual implementation of the operation in the field'.[17] These two elements, together with the powers conferred on the transitional authority, can have significant bearing on the ease or difficulty of implementation, and the success of an operation overall. This is as true of peacekeeping as it is of international administration.

All operations, even those of indefinite duration, envisage an end state. How well defined that end state is, however, can vary significantly. In the case of UNTAES, it was clear from the outset that Eastern Slavonia would be returned to Croatia. It is also clear that East Timor will gain independence. UNMIK's aims, on the other hand, have been more ambiguous, reflecting the international community's own uncertainty about the future status of Kosovo. The interim administration has been mandated to promote 'substantial autonomy and self-government' (without, however, undermining the sovereignty and territorial integrity of Yugoslavia[18]) and to facilitate a political process to determine Kosovo's future status. Yet, fearing the consequences of further state fragmentation in the Balkans, the international community has been decidedly cool towards the one option – independence – that ethnic Albanians, the vast majority of the population, favour. While Kosovo Albanians recognise that they owe their present freedom to the NATO states that opposed the repressive Belgrade regime and, to that extent, have welcomed the interim administration, the lack of clarity about the end state has limited Albanian co-operation, encouraged the Albanians to maintain an underground military infrastructure[19] and set the stage for possible confrontation with international authorities in the future. The Serbs, similarly, have opposed any policy or decision by the international administration that they have interpreted as likely to contribute towards Kosovo's independence.

End state uncertainty has handicapped the operation in another respect. As long as Belgrade remains the formal sovereign authority in Kosovo, no international financial institution is able to lend to Kosovo.[20] Nor will any but the most fearless private investors risk their capital there – especially by buying state or socially owned enterprises whose ownership cannot be guaranteed.[21] Without loans or major private investment, Kosovo has been forced to rely largely on international aid, overseas remittances and some local taxes, which are hardly sufficient to meet the territory's enormous economic challenges. Moreover, these sources of revenue do not offer a basis for sustained economic development. Depressed economic conditions can be a breeding ground for further violence – as well as smuggling, prostitution and drug-trafficking – thus undermining the very goals which UNMIK is seeking to achieve.

Operational aims, then, can have implications for the ease or difficulty of implementation. Contextual factors are important, too. If propitious, they can render even the most challenging operations manageable. In the case of UNTAET, for instance, despite the clarity of the projected outcome, the UN encountered enormous difficulties in administering East Timor initially, largely because the UN was ill-prepared for the magnitude of the crisis and the rapid deployment it necessitated. Yet these difficulties were mitigated by the very favourable conditions that existed at the outset of the operation. The local population for the most part welcomed the UN and supported the mission's aims; the Indonesian armed forces and local militia had withdrawn across the border, making it possible to provide reasonable security; and there was only one interlocutor – the National Council of Timorese Resistance (CNRT) – that the international community had to negotiate with initially (as opposed to numerous, competing factions).[22]

Similarly in Eastern Slavonia, one of the most fiercely contested battlegrounds of the Yugoslav wars, something that would have been an impossible task in the recent past – the peaceful re-absorption of Serb-held territory into Croatia – was made easier by the objective conditions that prevailed there at the time of the

UN administration. In a series of bold military offensives (Operation Flash in May 1995 and Operation Storm in August 1995), Croatia had regained possession of other Serb-held territories, and by the autumn of 1995 was threatening to recapture Eastern Slavonia, the last Serb-held enclave, in the same manner. Meanwhile Belgrade, eager to improve its relations with the West, showed no willingness to come to the defence of the Croatian Serbs. Under the circumstances, the Serbs, who had resisted Croatian authority for four years, concluded that they had little choice now but to negotiate a settlement for limited autonomy with Zagreb and to co-operate with the UN, whose operation was seen to offer them the best opportunity to safeguard their interests.[23]

By contrast, initial conditions in Bosnia were not at all conducive to fulfilling the aims of the operation there. None of the warring parties was satisfied with the outcome of the Dayton negotiations, much of which had been conducted over their heads and behind their backs.[24] And the absence of a decisive military victory by any of the warring parties constrained the architects in formulating treaty terms which all of them would accept. As a result, a highly unstable compromise was achieved which sought to satisfy both the separatist tendencies of the Bosnian Serb leadership and the integrationist aspirations of the Bosniac (Muslim) and, to a lesser degree, Croat leadership by establishing a weak federal state consisting of separate national entities: the Federation of Bosnia and Herzegovina and the Republika Srpska.[25] Moreover, the constitutional requirements for consensus that underpin the work of the Parliamentary Assembly and the Presidency – a consensus designed to protect the 'vital interests' of the ethnic parties – allow the more intransigent elements among them to thwart the effective functioning of the central government.[26] Similar requirements for consensus, it is worth noting, contributed to the collapse of the Yugoslav federation in the 1980s. [27]

Some circumstances, therefore, would appear to be more favourable to international administration than others. Where the operational aims are well defined and attract broad support among the local population (as they do in East Timor), or where the contextual factors limit the opportunities for resistance (as in Eastern Slavonia), the administrative authority enjoys distinct advantages. There are, of course, many other factors that contribute to the success of an operation – not the least of which is the design of the administration, the resources made available to it and the conduct of the administrative authority on the ground. All the same, if the authority is not endowed with the right objective conditions, it will be limited in what it can achieve.

The tendency of policy-makers is to view the facts on the ground that form the parameters of an operation as a given constraint. Yet international administration often follows on from prior and extensive international engagement in a region. The extent to which outside powers can shape the objective conditions is therefore sometimes greater than imagined. For instance, it was pressure from the Clinton administration that was largely responsible for bringing to a halt the Bosniac-Croat offensive in October 1995 – an offensive that the administration initially supported and which by early October had reduced Serb control of Bosnian territory from 70 to 50 percent. Had the Bosniac-Croat forces been allowed to rout the Bosnian Serbs (as they might have been able to do), the terms of the peace settlement would perhaps have been very different. However, with the US Congress poised to lift the arms embargo against Bosnia – which risked creating a rift between the US and its Alliance partners, Britain and France, and thus embarrassing the administration in the run-up to a presidential election – the Clinton administration sought to end the fighting and achieve a diplomatic settlement as quickly as possible.[28] To the minds of many Western leaders, moreover, a stable peace in Bosnia required establishment of a rough parity between the antagonists, albeit (arguably) at the price of compromising the efficacy of the post-conflict regime that the international community was to establish. Even Richard Holbrooke, the US envoy chiefly responsible for negotiating the Dayton agreement, would later question whether that price was not too high: 'Had we known then that the Bosnian Serbs would have been able to defy or ignore so many of the key provisions of the peace agreement in 1996 and 1997, the negotiating team might not have opposed such an attack [on Banja Luka]'.[29]

External actors, then, are sometimes in a position to mould the strategic and political backdrop to an international administration. But states have generally been more concerned with whether and how to intervene than with what to do in the aftermath of an intervention. The latter has not always been given sufficient consideration (although the Russians certainly grasped the point – which underlay their quick deployment to Pristina airport in the hope of establishing a zone of influence in Kosovo following the cessation of hostilities.)[30] Such lack of far-sightedness, we will see, also has consequences for operational efficiency.

Actors and Structures

What all contemporary international administrations have in common – and what distinguishes them from some of the earlier experiences of a similar nature – is the multiplicity of actors involved. Under both the League of Nations mandatory system and the UN trusteeship system, a state, a group of states or the world organisation itself could be designated to administer a territory, but it was common practice to appoint a single state to play this role. Thus the United Kingdom administered the British Cameroons, Tanganyika and Togoland; France the French Cameroons and French Togoland; Belgium Rwanda-Urundi; Australia New Guinea; and New Zealand Western Samoa under both the League and UN systems.[31] The exceptions have been the Saarland (Germany), where the League assumed responsibility for administration of the territory from 1920 to 1935; Nauru, where the United Kingdom, Australia and New Zealand were the administering authorities from 1947 to 1968, with Australia acting for them; and West New Guinea/West Irian (Indonesia), which the UN administered briefly as the United Nations Temporary Executive Authority (UNTEA) after the Netherlands' withdrawal from the territory in 1962.

Today the situation is different. In a post-colonial age, it would be politically unacceptable to entrust responsibility for the administration of a territory to a single state, even if elaborate accountability mechanisms were established. Moreover, the costs of administration would likely be too great for a single state to bear. As a result this function is performed by the UN or (in the case of Bosnia) the Peace Implementation Council (PIC) – an *ad hoc* coalition of states and organisations enjoying the endorsement of the UN.[32] The broad representative character of these administrative or supervisory bodies lends vital legitimacy to operations of this kind (although, of course, some states exert more influence than others in the context of these multilateral arrangements).

In all past cases, even where the United Nations has been the administrative authority, the number of other actors involved has been relatively few. In Kosovo, by contrast, four organisations function informally as co-principals. These are the Organisation for Security and Co-operation in Europe (OSCE), the European Union, the NATO-led Kosovo Force (KFOR) and the United Nations – the last involving a large number of its specialised agencies and departments: the UN High Commissioner for Refugees (UNHCR), the World Food Programme (WFP), the UN Children's Fund (UNICEF), the Human Rights Office, the UN Development Programme (UNDP), the World Health Organisation (WHO), the Department of Peacekeeping Operations (DPKO) and the Office for the Co-ordination of Humanitarian Affairs (OCHA), among others. Many international or regional organisations also play important supporting roles: the World Bank, the International Monetary Fund (IMF), the International Criminal Tribunal for the former Yugoslavia (ICTY), the International Committee of the Red Cross (ICRC), the Council of Europe and the International Labour Organisation (ILO). In addition, many states maintain missions in Kosovo that are very influential players, often giving direction to international policy or undertaking initiatives unilaterally. Scores of non-governmental organisations are active on the ground as well.

The reasons for this proliferation of actors are threefold. First, there simply are many more international or regional organisations and agencies now than in the past, and, in the European theatre especially, competition among them means that they are under constant pressure to establish new competences and deny opportunities to potential rivals. Second, in some cases – notably Kosovo and East Timor – no other local public administration or authority existed at the time that could provide even the most basic services, and there were also few local individuals qualified to perform many of them. Hence, there has been a need for the wholesale importation of governmental infrastructures. Finally, new sensibilities mean that the international community is now expected to deliver more than transitional authorities did in the past. Environmental protection, privatisation and the promotion of civil society are but a few of the new 'services' expected, each requiring skill bases that often only specialised agencies possess.

The multiplicity of actors creates problems of co-ordination similar to those that have handicapped complex peacekeeping operations. But it also has implications for the *structure* of international administrations. Bosnia is perhaps the most extreme case: differences among so many external actors resulted in a highly atomised and unwieldy administrative framework, with consequences for the effectiveness of the operation. As Marcus Cox observes:

> *Differences in interest among the different international actors during the Bosnian war have been reflected in a cumbersome international structure in the post-war phase. Early proposals for an international presence powerful enough to take control over reconstruction and institution building came to nothing. Mistrust between American and European policy-makers made it impossible to bring the intervention within a single institutional structure.*[33]

Consequently, there is no single, integrated body responsible for administration of the international effort in Bosnia. Rather, numerous institutions operate autonomously under the general direction of the High Representative. And, just as the High Representative has had little power as against the local national authorities (at least initially), so he has very limited authority over international agencies. The Dayton agreement is very explicit about this: 'The High Representative shall respect their autonomy within their spheres of operation while as necessary giving general guidance to them about the impact of their activities on the implementation of the peace settlement'.[34] The High Representative's role is merely to 'co-ordinate' the activities of the civilian organisations and agencies.[35] Donor states, multilateral aid agencies and non-governmental organisations may thus set their own objectives and pursue their own strategies, advised but not directed by the High Representative.

What this has meant, in the early days especially, is a lack of policy coherence among the major actors, even to the extent of agencies occasionally working at cross-purposes. For instance, disagreements over the appropriateness of political conditionality as an instrument for promoting compliance with the Dayton accord has sometimes set the World Bank apart from its partner agencies. Constrained by institutional mandates, the Bank has been reluctant to be interventionist in support of what it perceives to be overtly political objectives.[36] In Mostar in 1996, for instance, the Bank ignored EU efforts to make aid conditional on co-operation between the Croats and the Bosniacs and offered the Bosniac authorities assistance for the reconstruction of a hydroelectric plant, prompting the EU to abandon its policy.[37] Similarly, when the Office of the High Representative began to play a more assertive role in pushing for the return of refugees and displaced persons, it faced resistance from the UNHCR (the lead agency in this area), which had concerns about evicting individuals who were occupying the homes of returnees.[38] 'There has to be a homogeneous decision-making body to work through such a crisis as Bosnia was and is', Michael Steiner, the Deputy High Representative, would argue just before he left office in June 1997.[39]

The international community has apparently learned from the difficulties of Bosnia. UNMIK and UNTAET have brought the many different actors in under a single umbrella. In the case of Kosovo, a pillared structure has been established, with each of the principal agencies or organisations operating under the authority of the Special Representative of the UN Secretary-General (SRSG) – first Bernard Kouchner and then Hans Haekkerup – who is also the Transitional Administrator (TA). The civil administration as originally designed was composed of four main components, each with lead responsibility in a particular area: the United Nations (civil administration), UNHCR (humanitarian issues), OSCE (institution-building) and the EU (reconstruction). The components rely on the capabilities and expertise of the lead organisation, as well as those of various other international organisations and agencies, but answer ultimately to the SRSG, the 'highest international civilian official in Kosovo'.[40] Yet some of these components serve many masters (the OSCE, for instance, also receives policy and adminis-

Figure 1 UNMIK Joint Interim Administrative Structure (as of May 2001)

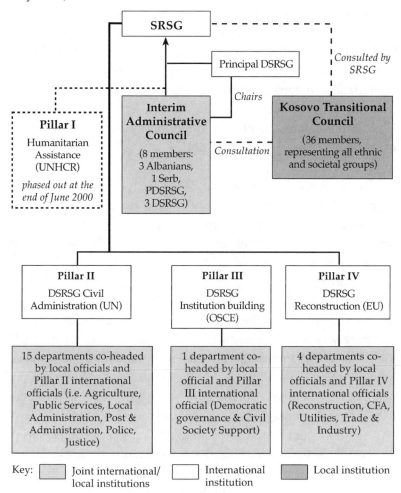

trative advice from its Permanent Council and Chairperson-in-Office), and UN officials complain that these components still have too much autonomy, and too much time is spent arguing about relative responsibilities.[41] In the case of UNTAET, where the mission is entirely in the hands of the SRSG (Sergio Vieira de Mello), and far fewer regional organisations are involved, a greater degree of integration has been achieved.

Integration does not always extend to the inclusion of multinational forces, however. In both Bosnia and Kosovo – largely at the insistence of the US government, whose soldiers serve there –

the multinational forces are under the authority of a NATO commander. Prompt and effective enforcement of civil authority has
not always been assured as a result. In Bosnia this was particularly
evident soon after the Dayton agreement came into effect, when
Carl Bildt, the High Representative at the time, was powerless to
order the deployment of troops to prevent Serb leaders using
intimidation to force a scorched-earth exodus of Bosnian Serbs
from the Sarajevo suburbs. As the Dayton agreement states: 'The
High Representative shall have no authority over the IFOR [Im-
plementation Force] and shall not in any way interfere in the
conduct of military operations or the IFOR chain of command'.[42]
(The fragmented nature of the NATO-led operation has only
aggravated this problem. For, while some troops have lent their
support to law enforcement – for instance, in the apprehension of
war-crimes suspects – their readiness to engage has been at the
discretion of each national command.) By contrast, UNTAES, a
contemporaneous operation, combined civil and military authority
in a single person – the Transitional Administrator, Jacques Paul
Klein – which clearly enhanced the effectiveness of the operation.[43]
Not only was the TA able to order the rapid deployment of UN
forces (as he did, for instance, when Serb paramilitaries (Scorpions)
refused at first to demilitarise) but the civilian and military components of the operation worked closely together, pooling resources
to meet the logistical and administrative needs of the mission.[44]
With UNTAC and UNTAET, similarly, the military component of
the mission was placed under the authority of the SRSG.

In all of this it needs to be remembered that some of the more
contingent aspects of an operation can sometimes make a critical
difference, rendering it difficult to generalise about formulae for
success. With UNTAES, for instance, important as the integrated
structure was, the fact that the operation was headed by a senior
American diplomat who was also a major-general in the US Air
Force Reserve contributed significantly to the mission's success in
a number of areas. It ensured that the operation would have
political and resource support from a very important quarter. It
also ensured that the operation would have credibility in the eyes
of the local parties.[45] (Croatia's President Franjo Tudjman had
indicated, moreover, that he would only accept the establishment

Figure 2 Structure of UNTAET and ETTA

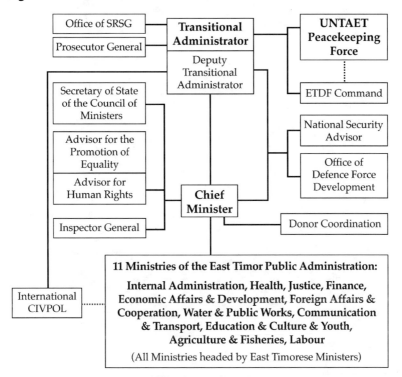

of a UN mission if it were headed by an American.[46]) Similarly, the fact that the force commander was from a NATO country (Belgium) facilitated the development of strong co-operative relations with the NATO-led Implementation Force based in neighbouring Bosnia, reflected in the contingency plans that provided for NATO to come to the assistance of UNTAES in the event of an emergency. In addition, regular overflights by NATO fixed-wing aircraft sent a strong signal of NATO/IFOR support to all parties concerned.[47] These features of the operation, while not necessarily unique to UNTAES, are not easily replicated for all international administrations.

Chapter 2

International Administration in Practice

International administration encompasses a broad range of activities – broader, we have seen, than complex peacekeeping. Some of these activities relate to immediate needs, such as the establishment of a secure environment and the delivery of humanitarian aid. Others are directed towards the longer-term requirements of a territory, including economic reconstruction and political institution-building. These twin imperatives can come into conflict with one another as international authorities, eager to achieve demonstrable progress in the short term, may fail to attach sufficient importance to ensuring sustainable results beyond the transitional period. The more fundamental challenge for an international administration, however, is the sheer number of functions it must perform, many of them simultaneously and with great urgency, and the difficulty of identifying the priority tasks as the situation on the ground evolves.

Not all the functions of international administration will necessarily be carried out by the international authorities themselves. Even in cases of direct governance, international administrators may harness local capacity for that purpose, as the UN did in Eastern Slavonia. But where such capacity does not exist, or where it may be considered imprudent to empower local authorities (for instance, where political competition threatens to compromise the integrity of service delivery for minority communities), the international administration may prefer not to devolve very much responsibility, at least initially.

The chief functions of an international administration can be grouped into six broad categories of activity:

i.   Establishing and maintaining public order and internal security, including the protection of human rights;
ii. Providing humanitarian assistance;
iii. Resettling refugees and internally displaced persons;
iv. Performing basic civil administrative functions;
v.   Developing local political institutions, including holding elections to these institutions, and building civil society;
vi. Economic reconstruction.

Some of these functions represent traditional post-conflict reconstruction efforts: notably the delivery of humanitarian aid and the resettlement of refugees. Notwithstanding the fact that every crisis generates its own special challenges, the novelty of these functions thus lies less in the activities themselves than in the difficulties posed by integrating them into a larger framework of operations. Other functions, or aspects of them, while not necessarily unique to international administrations, represent more recent features of peace operations, and they are discussed briefly below.

Establishing and Maintaining Public Order and Internal Security

Public order and internal security are the *sine qua non* of civil rule and, by extension, of the international administration of a territory. In war-torn societies, even if the guns have been silenced, individuals may still live in fear of reprisal or may suffer persecution by a police force or judiciary beholden to factional leaders. Or, in the absence of any local police force at all, anarchy may prevail and organised crime flourish. Establishing and maintaining public order and internal security are thus among the most important functions for the United Nations and other international bodies engaged in administering and reconstructing societies emerging from civil wars.

International administrations are responsible for order and security in a territory to a far greater degree than 'peace-support' operations have been in the past. Missions today may have a mandate not only to monitor local law-enforcement activities but also to establish local police forces where none exist; to train local police officers, to ensure that their activities are compliant with international standards for democratic policing; to investigate alleged human-rights abuses by local law-enforcement personnel; to restructure local police forces, so as to rationalise their size and achieve an ethnic composition reflecting the community they serve; to monitor judicial proceedings and detention centres; and in some cases themselves to carry out the task of policing – what is known as 'executive authority policing'. International civilian police (CIVPOL) may be helped to carry out these activities by, among others, peacekeeping troops, international judges and prosecutors, penal experts and human-rights officers.

An international administration's effectiveness at these tasks is highly dependent on four factors: readiness, resources, the nature of the mandate and, most crucially, the extent of support from international security forces deployed on the territory.

Readiness

The first six to twelve weeks after a ceasefire or peace agreement is perhaps the most critical period for establishing a secure environment and the credibility of an international peace force, both civilian and military.[1] Slowness to deploy creates an opportunity for spoilers to cause serious and sometimes irreparable damage to a mission.[2] For instance, the transfer of the Serb-held Sarajevo suburbs to Federation control (originally scheduled to take place 45 days after implementation of the Dayton accord was initiated) had to be postponed because there were too few international police monitors on hand, and the delay gave the Bosnian Serb authorities time to prepare a forced evacuation, ransacking and torching homes as they left.[3] (For its part, the Bosnian government did little to encourage the Serb residents to stay.) The monitors' personnel strength did not rise above 1,600 – as against a target number of 1,721 – until July 1996.[4] In Kosovo, too, although KFOR was responsible for ensuring public safety in the initial phase of operations, sluggish police deployment meant that, five months into the operation, UNMIK police were totally reliant on the military for law enforcement in three out of five regions.[5] In the absence of international police, local mafia were able to take control of socially owned enterprises throughout the territory, including the Grand Hotel in Pristina.

The difficulty, in part, is that many contributing countries do not have police officers readily available for service overseas; unlike soldiers, police officers are likely to be actively engaged at home. Also, recruitment for police operations – in contrast to military deployments – often cannot begin before the operation has been authorised. Thus, while the need for a police mission in Bosnia was evident from at least the start of the Dayton negotiations in mid-November 1995, the UN could not start recruiting for the operation until after the adoption on 21 December of Security Council Resolution 1035, which authorised the establishment of the International Police Task Force (IPTF).[6] In Kosovo, similarly, serious planning did not begin until after the military campaign had ended, by which point it was clear that the UN, as opposed to the OSCE, would be given responsibility for policing.[7]

Resources

Not only are police officers slow to deploy, they are also not available in sufficient numbers, because most states do not have reserve police capacity. This is true especially of Great Britain and, to lesser extent, the United States, which have no national police forces and must seek recruits from small, resource-scarce local police forces or from among retirees.[8] Moreover, the police that are made available do not always have the necessary qualifications. In East Timor, even officers who had passed the UN's Selection Assistance Team tests in their native countries were discovered to lack the necessary English-language and driving skills when they arrived in theatre a few months later – a problem known as 'slippage'. And, because the mission has been short-staffed, commissioners have come under pressure not to repatriate officers who do not meet the minimum standards.[9] In Kosovo, on the other hand, some police have been ordered home, but their countries have sometimes refused their return.[10]

There are difficulties, too, for police officers who come from autocratic regimes that themselves do not conform to international human-rights standards, and this creates problems of both effectiveness and credibility. International police are also often given insufficient logistical support. In Bosnia, the UN was asked to transfer all its assets to IFOR, which meant that the IPTF suffered severe shortages of transport vehicles, communications equipment and interpreters – shortages that plagued the operation well into its second year.[11]

Mandate

Like the international administrations of which they are a part, police missions can be distinguished on the basis of the degree of executive authority that they possess. In Cambodia and Bosnia, international police authority was limited largely to monitoring, investigating, advising, training and restructuring the local police forces. In such cases, responsibility for maintaining a safe and secure environment, as well as for implementing reforms, rests ultimately with the local parties themselves, and the result has often been unsatisfactory. UNTAC police were only given power of arrest in January 1993 – too late to be effective – and for a long time the only weapon at the disposal of the IPTF was 'decertification' of local police officers, dismissal being reserved for use by the local authorities alone. Obstruction by these authorities has meant that progress towards the integration of Bosniac and Croat police forces, and the recruitment of minority police officers in both entities, has been achieved very slowly in many cases and only as a result of enormous pressure from the IPTF, the High Representative and the Stabilisation Force (SFOR), the successor to IFOR.[12]

In Kosovo and East Timor, by contrast, where no formal institutions existed after the war to maintain order, CIVPOL has for the first time assumed full responsibility for law enforcement – with the assistance of international peacekeepers – pending the establishment of local police forces. Its effectiveness has been hampered mostly by problems of readiness and resources (including unsuitable police officers), exacerbated by the fact that CIVPOL is often also required to perform numerous non-policing tasks, such as traffic control and guarding banks and money transfers.[13] Difficulties have also arisen from the use of mixed national contingents – a practice the multinational peacekeeping forces do not employ – when, for instance, problems of communication have threatened to jeopardise the safety of officers using firearms.[14]

Peace-enforcement support

Problems of readiness and resources – personnel shortages especially – mean that an international administration is likely to be
dependent on the support of international security forces for establishing and maintaining internal security, at least initially. However, in the absence of a unified, cohesive structure under the
authority of a transitional administrator, that support may not
always be forthcoming. In Bosnia, heavily armed IFOR troops long
resisted pressures – from the High Representative and the International Criminal Tribunal for the former Yugoslavia (ICTY) – to
arrest indicted war criminals. As a result, not a single arrest was
made for the first 18 months, and this helped to perpetuate a
climate of insecurity, especially among ethnic minorities.[15] IFOR's
passivity reflected, in particular, US government apprehension
about putting its soldiers in harm's way. Indeed, Richard Holbrooke was under strict instructions to negotiate a narrow role for
IFOR at Dayton that excluded any police functions.[16]

In Kosovo and East Timor the situation has been very different: there international peacekeepers have been given explicit
responsibility for the maintenance of internal security, notably in
the first phase of operations. Resolution 1244 tasks KFOR with
'establishing a secure environment ... and ensuring public safety
and order until the international civil presence can take responsibility for this task'. KFOR has taken this responsibility seriously,
engaging in community patrolling, criminal investigations and
other policing activities, as well as conducting joint security operations with UNMIK police – though some national contingents
perform these tasks more diligently than others: a reflection, again,
of the fragmented nature of troop deployments in NATO-led
operations. Despite its willingness to execute policing functions,
KFOR failed to prevent the wave of violence that swept the
province as returning Albanian refugees took revenge on the Serb
and other minority populations,[17] and failed to prevent Serb mili-
tants from effecting a *de facto* partition of the town of Mitrovica
along the Ibar River.[18]

Providing security requires more than effective policing. Among
other things, this needs to be complemented by the establishment

of an effective court system able to conduct fair and impartial trials. Yet, in war-torn societies, bias or intimidation may influence the judgement of local judges (if these even exist in sufficient numbers), and some cases may be considered too 'hot' to touch. The appointment of international judges, with the power to select cases in which they wish to be involved, can serve as a check against abuse or timidity, as it has with some belated success in Kosovo and East Timor.[19] An issue for executive administrations, however, is which law to apply? Existing law may be unacceptable to the local population (as the Serbian Criminal Code was to Kosovo Albanians), and, even if acceptable, will not necessarily be known to the international police, judges, lawyers and prosecutors responsible for implementing it. In the early days of a transitional authority, especially, soldiers enforcing the law and administering justice will therefore tend to rely on their own national norms and conventions, and this can sometimes produce significant disparities in practice.[20] There is thus growing support among international police officers for the elaboration of a generic criminal code, in which mission personnel could receive pre-training, which could be used by transitional authorities pending the establishment of a local legal regime.[21]

Another task that is important for internal security is demili-tarising a region, including disposing of weapons in civilian hands, and reintegrating ex-combatants. In Eastern Slavonia, demilitarisa-tion was achieved through the surrender of heavy weapons be-longing to the local Serb forces or the redeployment of those forces to Yugoslavia, and through a successful weapons buy-back pro-gramme financed by the Croatian government that aimed at the removal of lighter weapons.[22] In Kosovo, there has been greater resistance to demilitarisation – notwithstanding the Kosovo Liber-ation Army (KLA)'s surrender of a large quantity of its arms initially[23]– and KFOR and UNMIK police have had to conduct 'search and seize' operations throughout the territory as a result. Efforts have also focused on demobilising and reintegrating KLA ex-combatants – for which purpose the Kosovo Protection Corps (KPC), a civilian emergency service agency, has been established, thus generating employment for thousands of formerly armed guerrillas under the eyes of international observation (although many ex-combatants see the KPC as a Kosovo Army in waiting). In East Timor, where pro-Indonesian militias continue to pose a threat from across the border, the decision was taken to create the East Timor Defence Force (ETDF), a light infantry force made up in large part of demobilised soldiers from Falintil, the armed wing of the Timorese resistance movement.[24] (The World Bank and International Organisation for Migration have undertaken to reintegrate the Falintil members who have not joined the ETDF.[25]) Finally, Bosnia has been subject to seemingly contradictory policies: alongside a series of arms-reduction measures, the controversial decision was taken to 'train and equip' the Federation army so as to establish a more level playing field in relation to the Bosnian Serb and Croat forces.[26] While this has arguably helped to reduce the threat of military domination by any one national group, it has also made it more difficult to achieve integration of the three armies or, more modestly, a state-level defence policy – a requirement for the establishment of a unitary state and for Bosnia's eventual membership in the family of European institutions.[27]

Resettling Refugees and Internally Displaced Persons

Public security is intimately related to the resettlement of refugees and the internally displaced, particularly in the context of intra-state conflicts, where the migration of civilians is often not an accident but a deliberate aim of combatants who seek to achieve ethnic homogeneity on the territory they control. Among the cases under consideration in this study, the problem in Bosnia has been the most acute: some 2.2 million people out of a total pre-war population of 4.3 million were forcibly displaced during the war, 1 million to locations within the country and 1.2 million abroad.[28]

Although Annex 7 of the Dayton accord establishes the rights of all displaced individuals to return to their homes of origin and requires the parties to the agreement to ensure that these individuals are permitted to return in safety and without risk of harassment, intimidation, persecution or discrimination,[29] the impunity that war criminals long enjoyed on the territory has been an obstacle to significant minority returns. It was not until mid-1997, when SFOR troops first began to arrest indicted war criminals and, with IPTF, to dismantle para-state intelligence structures, that minorities began to feel secure enough to return to their homes.[30] At the same time the OHR began to play a more assertive role in pushing for returns through the newly established Refugee Return Task Force (RRTF).[31] Today, even towns that experienced some of the fiercest fighting and most thorough 'ethnic cleansing' – Žepče, Kiseljak and Vitez in Central Bosnia, and Bijeljina, Prijedor and Srebrenica in Republika Srpska – have seen accelerating rates of minority returns, with restructured local police forces increasingly playing a role in ensuring the returnees' security.[32] Contextual factors are relevant here, too, especially to Central Bosnia. The advent in January 2000 of a new Croatian government, unwilling to continue the Tudjman government's policy of supporting the militancy of Bosnian Croats, has left the latter more dependent on international aid, and thus more responsive to international demands – a demonstration of the impact that regional dynamics can have on efforts to administer war-torn territories[33]– notwithstanding moves by the Bosnian Croats in March 2001 to challenge the Dayton framework and establish a 'temporary Croat self-government'.

Two additional factors have had a significant bearing on the incidence of returns – factors that are relevant more generally to transitional authorities' efforts to resettle displaced persons. The first is the availability of economic resources and social services. In order to attract and maintain returnees, it is necessary to provide them with adequate jobs, education, health care and other social services at the local level.[34] It was in part the failure of the Tudjman government to furnish such resources – for instance, the unwillingness of the government to provide economic assistance to Eastern Slavonia – that discouraged Serbs from remaining in the region.[35] (The OSCE estimates that between mid-1996 and July 1997 the number of Serbs in the Croatian Danube region fell from 109,800 to 62,800, but reliable figures are not available.)[36] And in Bosnia, delays in donor funding in 1999 led to a reversal of resettlement gains, as some returnees, who had waited for assistance for months, were forced to return to their war-time place of refuge before the onset of winter.[37]

The second factor is a comprehensive legal framework, properly enforced, that ensures the restitution of property to its legitimate owners (or to its prior occupants, since a clear determination of ownership may be difficult to establish in the case of socially owned property or where there are rival property claims, as there are in East Timor).[38] More than property legislation may be required for this purpose. In Croatia, citizenship laws discriminate against former Serb residents who fled during the war (many of them to Bosnia), and their presence in Republika Srpska – some 35,000 of them as of October 2000 – constitutes a serious obstacle to Bosniac and Croat minority returns to that entity.[39] Of course, even with the proper legislation in place, organised resistance by local political elites may obstruct returns, with delays in the processing of documents, requests for unauthorised fees or the failure to implement laws altogether. In Bosnia obstruction has meant that five years after the war the average rate of implementation of applications for repossession of property, although rising, had not exceeded 21 percent.[40] Continuous international monitoring and pressure – including pressure on local authorities to evict residents in cases of illegal or multiple occupancy – are thus essential to ensure the integrity of the minority return process, although it is now accepted that tens of thousands of refugees and internally displaced persons may never return, having established new lives for themselves elsewhere.[41]

Performing Basic Civil Administrative Functions

The most distinctive feature of transitional authorities is the establishment and management of interim administrative structures with wholesale responsibility for implementing public policy and delivering essential public services – the core functions of a government. While only in Kosovo and East Timor has it been necessary to create and manage such structures, all international administrations have at least very extensive oversight responsibility of local administrative structures. International civil administration is not entirely without precedent – the League of Nations administered the German Saarland for 15 years (1920–35), and, we have seen, the United Nations administered Dutch West New Guinea in 1962–3 – but only rarely in the past have collective organisations, in contrast to colonial powers, assumed such broad responsibility.[42]

In Bosnia international authorities have relied chiefly on local governmental bodies for the performance of administrative functions. Difficulties have arisen because the local authorities have often been more concerned with the pursuit of partisan gains than with general welfare. In Republika Srpska, some of the parties have been so determined to prevent the functioning of common institutions that they have been willing to deny their citizens rights as basic as freedom of travel outside their own territory. Were it not for the decision of the High Representative to require adoption of a common license plate for Bosnia and Herzegovina – one that did not betray the vehicle-owner's place of residence – individuals today might still be too fearful to move beyond the relative safety of their entities.[43] The few administrative bodies in Bosnia that have performed competently – notably the Independent Media Commission and the Central Bank – have been neither international nor local bodies but, rather, hybrid institutions run by internationals with the participation of members of the local community selected by the transitional authorities for their ability to perform their duties impartially.[44] These institutions have thus become delinked from nationalist politics.

Elsewhere various forms of 'joint implementation' have become the norm, in which responsibility for administration is shared with and among the local parties. In Kosovo, after an initial six-month period in which UN authorities competed with local parallel structures, many controlled by the KLA, UNMIK established the Joint Interim Administrative Structure (JIAS), an important element of which are the 20 administrative departments responsible for the management and delivery of public services.[45] Each administrative department, along with four independent agencies, is co-directed by a Kosovar and a senior UNMIK international staff member.[46] Similar arrangements were devised for East Timor, where Timorese were selected to fill deputy positions in both the central administration in Dili and in the 13 districts, with the expectation that they would gradually replace the internationals at the helm. However, where political and ethnic competition has been fierce – as it has been in Kosovo – administrative competence has suffered under these arrangements. Most if not all of the departmental co-heads in Kosovo, whose positions are distributed among the major political parties and representatives of three minority communities (Serb, Bosniac and Turk), have been selected by the local leadership largely on the basis of partisan considerations.[47] The difficulties that have plagued 'Timorisation', by contrast, have had more to do with lack of training and experience among the local administrators. Notwithstanding the degree of joint administration achieved, in all contemporary cases of transitional rule, administrative authority resides ultimately with the SRSG or his representative. This raises important questions about 'ownership' of the transitional process that are discussed in the following chapter.

Developing Local Political Institutions

Transitional authorities are, by their nature, interim arrangements that envisage the eventual transfer of full responsibilities for governance to local authorities. For this it is often necessary to develop local political institutions, either because no formal structures exist or because international authorities may consider existing structures inadequate – notably, because they may be undemocratic, unrepresentative or incapable of implementing international obligations.

Building local political institutions and fostering a political culture conducive to democratic governance require considerable time and commitment on the part of local and international players, assuming such a policy programme can succeed at all. Yet, in the case of Bosnia, the architects of the Dayton agreement chose to put the process of political institution-building on the 'fast track': elections for state, entity and municipal offices were to be held six to nine months after the agreement came into force, and IFOR was to withdraw in 12 months.[48] The commitment to early deadlines in both cases threatened to undermine the goals that these policies were intended to support.

The importance attached to prompt elections partly reflected the Clinton administration's interest in being able to point to demonstrable progress in Bosnia on the eve of a US presidential election (indeed the OSCE, which was to supervise the Bosnian elections, was known locally as the Organisation to Save Clinton's Election).[49] But there were other less parochial reasons that recommended the accelerated pace to policy-makers. First, the Western powers wanted the local parties to accept responsibility for their own futures sooner rather than later, and hoped that, in the face of an impending Western withdrawal, they would appreciate the need to work together. Second, it was thought that the elections could serve as an instrument to blunt the forces of militant nationalism, since candidates opposed to reconciliation and integration might be seen now to be impediments to the delivery of Western aid. Moreover, refugees and internally displaced persons – many of them the targets of aggressive nationalism – were expected to vote in those municipalities where they had been registered before the war, and it was thought that this would dilute the influence of militant nationalists.[50]

The tight and inflexible deadline set by the Dayton accord, however, could and did have the opposite effect – a consequence that could have been foreseen. Six to nine months allowed too little time for new thinking to emerge that might produce a realignment of political forces. The knowledge that soldiers would depart in 12 months (another decision driven by the Clinton administration's concerns about re-election) only compounded the problem, even if Clinton later decided not to withdraw the troops. Voters uncertain about their future would be inclined to choose the safe option: to vote for the same nationalist parties that had 'protected' their interests during the war. And it would be difficult for the Western powers to challenge the legitimacy of the results issuing from their own elections; on the contrary, these served only to confer legitimacy on the very individuals, including presumed war criminals, who were viewed as impediments to peace and reconciliation, as has each election subsequently.[51] Even Richard Holbrooke, the chief architect of Dayton, would worry aloud about the implications of this logic on the eve of the September ballot: 'Suppose the election was declared free and fair [and those elected] were racists, fascists, and separatists who are publicly opposed to [peace and reintegration]? That is the dilemma.'[52]

Partly in reaction to the Bosnian experience, a more gradual approach has been taken to political institution-building in Kosovo and East Timor. In Kosovo, elections were not held until October 2000 (16 months after the establishment of the mission) and then only at the municipal level – which, in theory at least, gave time for more moderate political forces to gain ground lost to the KLA, and shifted attention away from some of the larger contentious issues, notably that of national self-determination, which threatened to drive a wedge between the local population and the international community. In East Timor, gradualism has been abetted by the local population's own wariness about elections,[53] the first of which UNTAET did not organise until 30 August 2001 for the purpose of electing 88 members to a constituent assembly to draft East Timor's constitution. The East Timorese have had very limited prior experience with balloting: the 1999 referendum on independence and the elections held after Portugal's withdrawal in 1975 were both marred by massive violence.

Tolerant though the populations of these territories have been of the gradualist approach to the creation of institutions of self-government, there has been palpable dissatisfaction with the interim power-sharing arrangements. In both Kosovo and East Timor, the UN set up consultative bodies – the Kosovo Transitional Council (KTC) and the National Consultative Council (NCC) respectively – to function as shadow parliaments alongside the joint administrative structures mentioned above.[54] In Kosovo, additionally, an Interim Administrative Council (IAC) – an eight-member advisory group made up of four UNMIK officials and four Kosovars (three Kosovo Albanian political leaders and an observer representative of the Kosovo Serb community) – was established to make recommendations to the SRSG to amend applicable law and frame new regulations, and to propose policy guidelines for the 20 administrative departments. In East Timor, district advisory councils were also created, and, under the auspices of the World Bank-managed Community Empowerment Programme (CEP), democratically elected village councils were established to make decisions concerning local development projects.[55]

Despite the creation of these consultative mechanisms, the local leaderships in both territories have expressed considerable frustration with the limited power they exercise and with what they see as a lack of seriousness by international officials about consultation – evident, for instance, in the failure to allow the NCC sufficient time to study proposed regulations.[56] This frustration should have been anticipated, and (especially in the case of East Timor, where the UN mission enjoyed broad support from the start) efforts to establish a more meaningful partnership with representatives of the local population could have been accelerated. In response to the frustration, Vieira de Mello replaced the NCC with the National Council (NC) on 14 July 2000 and established the 'Cabinet of the Transitional Government in East Timor'.[57] (These two bodies, in turn, were replaced by a Constituent Assembly and an all-Timorese Council of Ministers in September 2001.) The NC was more representative than the NCC and had the power to initiate, modify and recommend draft regulations; to amend regulations; and to call Cabinet members before it to answer questions regarding their respective functions. Cabinet members in turn were vested with 'executive authority' over the offices and departments that corresponded to their respective portfolios.[58] Council and Cabinet members were appointed, however, not elected. And, as with all these administrative structures, final authority resides with the Transitional Administrator. Although frustration has abated, the lack of resources available for the Transitional Government, in contrast to those provided to the UN mission, is a continuing source of consternation.

In Bosnia, where local leaders have exercised many of the powers of state from the outset, the High Representative has taken the opposite tack and sought increasingly to curb their authority through the exercise of peremptory powers awarded him by the Peace Implementation Council. At its meeting in Bonn in December 1997 the PIC empowered the High Representative to impose laws in the absence of a willingness of local governing parties to adopt them and to dismiss from office public officials whom the High Representative considers to be violating their obligations under the Dayton agreement.[59] The High Representative has exercised his 'Bonn powers' on more than 100 occasions, including, in the past year, to order a restructuring of the Constitutional Commissions in the Federation and the Republika Srpska parliaments; to establish a memorial site for the victims of the 1995 massacre at Srebrenica; to impose a package of new economic legislation, including amendments to pension and disability insurance laws in both entities so as to satisfy the conditions for the disbursement of

Figure 3 Decisions of the High Representative, 1997–2001

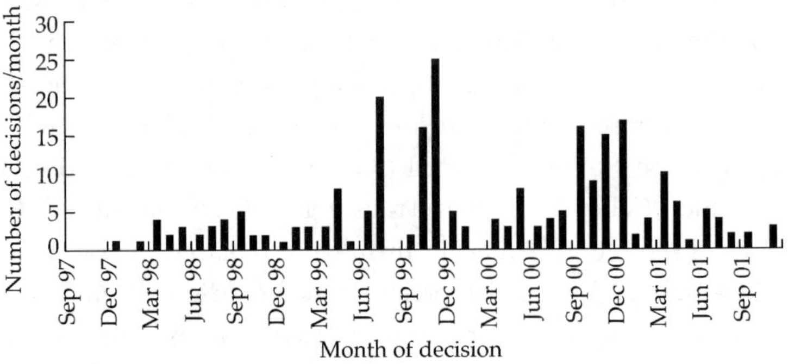

World Bank structural adjustment credits; and to establish an Independent Judicial Commission to help overcome opposition to judicial reform.

Additionally, since March 1998, the High Representative has dismissed, suspended or banned from public office over 70 elected officials, including mayors, presidents of municipal assemblies, cantonal ministers, delegates to the entity parliaments, a former prime minister of the Bosnian Federation (Edhem Bičakčić), the president of Republika Srpska (Nikola Poplasen) and a member of the Bosnian Presidency (Ante Jelavić).[60] Critics argue that these practices have been counterproductive – pointing out, for instance, that dismissed officials are often replaced by similarly oriented individuals – and that 'rule by decree' sets a poor example for the proper functioning of a democratic society.[61] We return to this question in the next chapter.

More than just the holding of elections and the establishment of consultative, legislative and/or executive bodies, political institution-building also entails political party capacity-building, the development and regulation of the mass media; the training of a professional, apolitical civil service; the development of an independent judiciary; support for non-governmental organisations and the promotion of civil society generally; the provision of technical assistance to parliamentary assemblies; and other related activities. More than any other feature of a transitional regime, institution-building has potentially far-reaching implications for the future political complexion of an administered territory.

Economic Reconstruction

Satisfactorily functioning local political institutions, and the rule of law in particular, are important not only for democratic self-government but also in relation to economic development – a basic requirement for the long-term viability of distressed territories. Where systematic corruption, cronyism and a non-functional judicial system are the norm, private investors are unlikely to be attracted to a region. In Bosnia these factors, together with excessively high taxes, cumbersome regulations and barriers to inter-entity trade, have discouraged inward capital flows.[62] In 2000 net foreign direct investment in Bosnia was a mere $117 million.[63] Indeed, virtually all economic growth since the end of the war is attributable to donor aid ($5.1 billion for the four-year period beginning in 1996). Without this external assistance, the United States Agency for International Development (USAID) estimates, Bosnia would not have exhibited annual double-digit growth rates since 1995 but rather a *negative* 1 percent.[64] To the extent that economic deprivation may be a source of renewed conflict, Bosnia cannot be said to be out of the woods yet.

Economic reconstruction in many cases is actually a misnomer. For international players do not generally seek to restore what existed before the devastating events – often an inefficient, statist system – but to transform the economy by privatising state-owned enterprises, building strong but not predatory public-sector institutions, eliminating barriers to trade and establishing investment-friendly tax regimes. The challenge for international administrators is thus a triple one: development, transition and physical reconstruction, each with its own conceptual framework and approach. (For one thing, the degree of acceptable state interference in the economy may differ depending on the approach.) This challenge is compounded by the fact that target territories will often have experienced a sharp deterioration of living standards – evidenced by higher poverty, inequality and unemployment – as a result of war.[65]

Overcoming this triple challenge necessitates a degree of co-ordination among external parties that can be difficult to achieve because of the inherent autonomy of the key actors involved: donor states, regional and international aid agencies, and development banks. These parties may be motivated by a variety of interests (not all mutually compatible) and constrained by their own norms and operating procedures. Yet co-ordination is important for reasons of efficiency, particularly in the case of conflict regions such as the Balkans, where several territories are facing similar and interconnected challenges. It is recognition of this fact that led some 40 states and organisations, on the EU's initiative, to establish the Stability Pact for South East Europe in June 1999. [66] However, the Pact, which has no funds of its own, has not defined itself in a way that would encourage major international donors to give it the central place it requires if it is to serve as a secretariat for overall assistance efforts in the region.[67]

Input from the target countries is also important for post-war economic recovery: programmes that reflect a territory's specific problems and preferences are more likely to succeed. This is one of the lessons that has been drawn from the experience of the Marshall Plan in the aftermath of the Second World War.[68] The difficulty arises when the strategic aims of the external actors are not shared by the local parties – who, for instance, may want to continue pursuing war objectives by peaceful means – and is further compounded when the external actors themselves disagree on what their strategic aims should be. Aid conditionality may help to gain the co-operation of these local parties but, like sanctions, can be a blunt and even counterproductive instrument – to the extent of inhibiting economic regeneration.[69]

Chapter 3

Critical Issues for International Administrations

The challenges that international authorities face in the context of administering war-torn territories highlight certain key issues – planning for complex operations, the difficulty of balancing international responsibilities and local demands for self-rule, international accountability and appropriate exit strategies – that have considerable bearing on the quality of international administration and its effectiveness. Not all of these issues are unique to transitional authorities; a number arise also in relation to peacekeeping operations, but they can be more acute for international administration, if only because the scale of the operation is much greater. Other issues *are* unique – especially those of a more political nature – and failure to appreciate their special character has created difficulties for the international authorities and sometimes has led to the adoption of unsuitable strategies.

Planning of Operations

The problems associated with planning operations, whether traditional peacekeeping or transitional administrations, are well known. Critical though the initial period is for the establishment of a mission's effectiveness – as we have already seen with respect to policing – it is generally not until very late that planning for a mission begins.[1] In the case of East Timor, it was clear as early as 5 May 1999, when the Indonesian government agreed to offer the East Timorese a referendum on independence, that the UN would have some role to play in the administration of the territory following the referendum. Yet almost no planning towards the establishment of a transitional administration was begun until very late in the process.[2] Moreover, planning was predicated on the assumption of a peaceful outcome and a phased transition, either to independence or to autonomy within Indonesia, that would be achieved with the co-operation of the Indonesian authorities and through existing administrative structures. None of this transpired – nor should it have been expected, given the open contempt for democratic norms shown by the Indonesian military and its allied militia.[3] Further difficulties were created as a consequence of the post-ballot violence and the need to deploy a multinational peace-keeping force. The mission was then transferred from the UN's Department of Political Affairs (DPA) to the Department of Peace-keeping Operations (DPKO). Since there is little capacity within the UN for cross-departmental planning, this resulted in the loss of most of DPA's knowledge input. Where collaboration across departments does exist, it is *ad hoc* and highly reliant for its success on personal networks, which, in this instance, were not well established.[4]

Another valuable source of knowledge and experience that is rarely drawn upon for planning purposes is the residents themselves. In the case of East Timor, the planning process for UNTAET involved no meaningful participation by East Timorese representatives. On 19 October 1999 Xanana Gusmão, President of the National Council of East Timorese Resistance (CNRT), forwarded proposals for a transitional administration to the UN, but these were effectively ignored; moreover, when the UN drew up its own plan, little effort was made to explain its logic and rationale to the East Timorese.[5] The structures of the three Balkans operations were also designed with little participation by the local parties, although earlier draft peace settlements, negotiated in consultation with the parties, did inform certain features of the international administrations in Bosnia and Kosovo. In the Balkans, however, the parties were not always receptive to the aims of the international authorities, which limited the scope of their contribution.

One key aspect of planning, the staffing of these missions, is particularly challenging for international administrations. Because of the relatively large size of transitional structures – of the civil administrative component especially – recruiting personnel is a mammoth task. And yet a single individual in New York was responsible for staffing the UN Mission in East Timor (UNAMET), the precursor to UNTAET, along with two other missions at the same time.[6] Sergio Vieira de Mello, the transitional administrator, thus had to make do with a skeletal Governance and Public Administration component for several months, fuelling local people's frustration with the international community's failure to make visible improvements in their lives, particularly in the districts outside the capital, which received less attention. Although a standard clause in UN contracts allows the UN Secretary-General to send staff wherever he wishes, senior qualified personnel are often not directed to serve in these missions. Transitional authorities thus lack people with the skills required to run a country. 'An inadequate number of UN personnel with inadequate means work long hours at fire-fighting and improvising, while trying to uphold the good name of the UN', Vieira de Mello has observed in this context.[7]

The absence of strategic planning, most notably again in the area of civil administration, is another of the chronic weaknesses of transitional administrations. In Kosovo, the first UNMIK strategic planning document was not produced until 5 December 1999, six months after the start of the mission. The second, a working draft issued on 18 March 2000, was so elaborate – 'a ceiling-to-floor laundry list', in the words of one UNMIK official – as to make it all but impossible to implement.[8] This is a reflection of the 'intra-mission creep' that may occur as a mission, and its constituent parts, take on new areas of responsibility. Efforts have subsequently been made to focus on a number of critical policy issues.[9] A similar process has been under way with respect to Bosnia, where the Peace Implementation Council, beginning with the Madrid Council meeting of December 1998, has been elaborating detailed implementation agendas, which have helped to focus the efforts of both international authorities and national governments working in support of them.[10]

Problems of planning thus occur at both the headquarters level (in the case of the United Nations) and the field level. The difficulties derive from a combination of factors, inadequate resources chief among them. The UN is simply not well enough resourced to be able to conduct the kind of contingency planning that is a hallmark of military organisations.[11] A single political desk officer in DPKO will typically serve as the 'focal point' for a mission as large as UNMIK or UNTAET, with some input from other personnel, and will have numerous other responsibilities as well. The consequences extend beyond the planning stage to day-to-day operations, as the Brahimi report notes:

> *In the current arrangements, compromises among compet-*
> *ing demands are inevitable and support for the field may*
> *suffer as a result. In New York, Headquarters-related tasks,*
> *such as reporting obligations to the legislative bodies, tend to*
> *get priority because Member States' representatives press for*
> *action, often in person. The field, by contrast, is represented*
> *in New York by an email, a cable or the jotted notes of a*
> *phone conversation. Thus, in the war for a desk officer's*
> *time, field operations often lose out and are left to solve*
> *problems on their own.[12]*

Organisational culture also militates against effective planning. The UN Secretariat is not encouraged by its member states to engage in early planning for transitional administrations, in part because of the political implications of such actions – which, from the stand-point of a target state, may seem very threatening indeed. With respect to East Timor, for instance, it would have meant planning for an eventuality that assumed the bad faith of Indonesia. In the case of *ad hoc* institutions, such as those responsible for the inter-national administration in Bosnia, the problems associated with planning may be even more acute, precisely because no established institutional infrastructure exists. The Office of the High Represen-tative takes its guidance from an informal body (the PIC and its Steering Board) that has no prior institutional and operational experience and acts only through the mandates of its members.

Building Local Capacity

Whatever the end state envisioned for a territory under inter-national administration – independence, autonomy or, in the case of 'collapsed' states, more effective governmental institutions – one primary objective of a transitional regime must be to empower the local population to manage its own affairs. Yet there is a temptation – especially in the early days of an operation, when emergency conditions prevail – for international authorities to rely principally, if not entirely, on international agencies and personnel for the implementation of their mandate. The danger, however, is that international authorities will be so concerned about adequate and efficient implementation, as they understand these aims, that they will be impervious to recipient input or will favour their own agencies and service-providers to the detriment of developing local capacity.[13]

The dilemma is very real. International organisations, sensitive to the sting of public opinion, particularly in the wake of the perceived peacekeeping failures of the 1990s – notably in Somalia, Bosnia and Rwanda – are concerned to avoid similar humiliation, and hence often prefer to take matters into their own hands. In the absence of local qualified individuals to perform civil administration functions, there may be little alternative. Moreover, there are not always sufficient checks and balances to justify simple budgetary support to local governments. Such concerns, however, can be (and sometimes are) exaggerated. In many cases it may be possible to devolve responsibility to the local population, insist on transparency and, as a safeguard, maintain control over the public purse, as was done in the case of UNTAET's Division of Health Services: the only 'governmental' division to be headed by an East Timorese nearly one year after the start of the operation.[14]

Early devolution of responsibility allows the local population to learn from their experiences under the watchful eye of international specialists who – given the vagaries of international assistance – may not be able to remain very long in a territory. (It is worth recalling that precipitous or premature withdrawal of administrative regimes in the context of decolonisation was one of the factors that contributed to instability in many newly independent Third World countries.[15]) Early devolution also helps to prevent the administrative equivalent of aid dependency, in which the local population becomes accustomed to international representatives making decisions for them, including some of the harder decisions that they can thus choose to ignore. Admittedly this is a problem even where international administration is more indirect, as it is in Bosnia. There the local parties have sometimes taken decisions that have been very popular with their constituents but which they knew would be overturned by the High Representative – for instance, the adoption of social welfare measures that the HR has found to be economically unsustainable. In this way local leaders have been able to occupy the political high ground and to blame the international community for their own failure to make good on their pledges.

As this example suggests, empowerment is a much harder policy to pursue where the local parties and international authorities are at cross-purposes. In such cases, should a transitional administrator defer to local preferences, however imprudent or even repugnant those preferences may seem? Or should a transitional administration instead use its extraordinary powers to seek to mould the society according to its own vision? What is clear is that where a transitional administrator serves as the UN Secretary-General's Special Representative, his or her first responsibility must be to ensure full compliance with the Security Council resolutions that established the interim administration and determined its mandate. (The High Representative has similar obligations with respect to implementing the civilian aspects of the Dayton accord.[16]) The language of the transitional administrators' regulations reflect this constraint: for instance, the regulation that established the East Timor's National Council stipulates: 'The final authority of the Transitional Administrator in exercising his responsibilities vested in UNTAET under Security Council Resolution 1272 (1999) … shall in no way be prejudiced by the provisions of this regulation'.[17] Thus where local preferences represent a patent violation of international legislation, or simply derogate from the authority of the TA, he or she has little choice but to override them. However, what constitutes compliance or implementation is often a matter of considerable debate, and a transitional administrator enjoys enormous discretion in this regard.

Consider the High Representative's 12 November 2000 decision on labour legislation adopted by the National Assembly of the Republika Srpska which would have provided generous compensation benefits to unemployed workers. Acting on the basis of guidance from the PIC, at its meeting in Brussels on 23–24 May, urging him to use his authority to remove obstacles to economic reform and to create the conditions for self-sustaining market-oriented economic growth,[18] the HR effectively rewrote the assembly legislation to reduce the level of benefits. In support of his decision, he observed that the legislation 'would have caused considerable financial difficulties to a large number of enterprises, thereby impeding the privatisation process and jeopardising current employment and the viability of enterprises all over the Republika Srpska'.[19] Is this an appropriate role for a transitional administrator to play? Should local authorities instead be allowed to suffer the consequences (or reap the rewards) of their choices, as freely elected representatives do elsewhere?

There is a fine line between ensuring compliance with a peace agreement and interference in the 'internal' affairs of a territory, even in the context of international administration. In Bosnia's case in particular, there would seem to be little doubt that the entities have authority over labour policy. The Constitution enumerates the responsibilities of the state institutions and makes clear that all other government functions and powers belong to the entities,[20] while the Constitution of the Republika Srpska explicitly grants the Republika Srpska the competence to regulate working relations.[21] Moreover, the provision of severance payments, generous or otherwise, does not violate any feature of the Constitution. Yet, in the absence of intervention by the HR (and this was one of 11 executive decisions relating to economic reform announced on 12 November), it is most unlikely that the local parties would adopt many of the measures necessary to enable Bosnia to make the transition from a donor-dependent to a self-sustaining economy. There clearly needs to be a balance between the competing demands of self-government, on the one hand, and international responsibilities, on the other. Where that balance is established will depend very much on the extent of the convergence of interests between local and international parties. However, it is important to bear in mind that international requirements, such as the creation of liberal economic mechanisms, may be as much matters of political choice as local preferences are.

One must also be wary of generalising about the scope for consultation and capacity-building on the basis of particular cases, valuable though 'lessons learned' exercises may be. One of the factors that may account for the slowness in devolving authority more quickly to the East Timorese was the tendency to apply the wrong lessons from the UN's operations in the Balkans. Many of UNTAET's initial core personnel were drawn from UNMIK, including Vieira de Mello, its head of mission, and a key lesson that some of them drew from the experience was the need to establish firm control over a territory from the outset.[22] But, whereas in Kosovo there were local forces that rivalled the UN (notably the KLA and Belgrade's surrogates among the Serbs), in East Timor the local leadership was entirely supportive of the UN's aims and could have been entrusted with more responsibility sooner. Vieira de Mello later acknowledged that his administration did not involve the East Timorese as fully as it should have. At the National Congress of the CNRT on 21 August 2000 he observed, 'While consultation and partnership were established early on, it became clear by April of this year that it was not sufficient ... Faced as we were with our own difficulties in the establishment of this mission, we did not, we could not involve the Timorese at large as much as they were entitled to.'[23]

Some of the problems arising from insufficient consultation are compounded by the tendency of international staff, in large missions especially, to detach themselves from the local population and from the realities of everyday life in the territories where they serve. Staff often do not live among the locals, cannot speak the local language and enjoy amenities not generally available to the locals – all of which may be understandable, but which nevertheless fosters mutual alienation and even resentment by the indigenous community. Comparisons with colonial administration may be unfair but they are easily called to mind in such circumstances.

Ruling by Decree

Using international power to impose particular outcomes also raises questions about the implications of such actions for the development of local political culture and institutions. Besides the risk of administrative dependency, there is also the danger that local populations, particularly those with little direct experience of democratic practices, will draw the wrong lessons from the more peremptory methods employed by transitional administrators.

This issue has perhaps been sharpest in Bosnia, where the gap between local and international aims has sometimes been very wide. There, for instance, the High Representative and other international parties have gone to great lengths to promote electoral outcomes which they thought represented the best chance for advancing the international agenda for Bosnia. Some of these actions have been so intrusive that in many other political contexts they would be seen as violating democratic principles. In one case, international efforts to undermine the leadership of Radovan Karadžić, the President of the militant nationalist Serbian Democratic Party (SDS), led the High Representative, first, to support Biljana Plavšić, President of the Republika Srpska, when she dissolved the SDS-controlled RS National Assembly in July 1997, and then to overrule the RS Constitutional Court when it found her action to be unconstitutional.[24] Even if the court's decision was a consequence of political pressures, as the High Representative maintained, there are clear dangers to overriding the constitutional order in this manner – and the inappropriateness of this action is further evidenced by the fact that Plavšić was later to be indicted for war crimes by the Hague Tribunal.

Freedom of expression has also been subject to severe restrictions in the interest of creating a politically neutral environment for the conduct of elections. On 6 September 1996 the Elections Appeals Sub-Commission (EASC), chaired by an international official possessing broad powers of interpretation of the election regulations, issued an advisory opinion that proscribed any statements by parties or their representatives that supported the territorial separation and independence of part of the country or referred to part of the country as sovereign territory. On the basis of this ruling the EASC fined the SDS $50,000 – not for having called into question the unity of Bosnia but for having 'continually stressed the substantial autonomy granted to Republika Srpska in the General Framework Agreement, to the total exclusion of any reference to the unity of Bosnia and Herzegovina'.[25] These and related incidents have led one critic to observe:

> *The ... democracy mission in Bosnia has become a grotesque*
> *parody of democratic principles.... We are teaching ... the*
> *virtues of democracy by showing ... that an outside power, if*
> *it possesses enough military clout, has the right to overrule*
> *court decisions, establish political purity tests for candidates*
> *for public office and suppress media outlets that transmit*
> *politically incorrect views.[26]*

The heavy-handed approach has not necessarily been very effective, either. The elections held in Bosnia on 11 November 2000 produced some gains for the moderate parties, but not the basic realignment of political forces which international efforts had been underwriting for the previous five years.[27] In Republika Srpska, the SDS emerged the clear victor, winning the Presidency, Vice-Presidency and a substantial number of seats in the National Assembly. In the Federation, the HDZ won an absolute majority among Croats. Among the war-time nationalist parties, only the Bosnian Muslim SDA lost ground – largely to the Social Democratic Party (SDP). Not only has international intervention in the political process failed to achieve a fundamental shift, it has sometimes even been counterproductive: in Bosnia's September 1998 elections strong international backing for reformist candidates – including pledges of additional financial assistance – appears to have contributed to their defeat, as some voters resented the intervention of the major powers.[28]

Indeed, it is questionable whether change that would allow Bosnia (or any other 'failed' state) to function as a self-sustaining liberal democracy can be achieved by means of administrative fiat. Ultimate success requires a 'will to democracy' among a people and its leaders, and an indigenous democratic culture alongside the formal democratic practices and institutions. Hence the vital importance of promoting the development of civil society – a clichéd sentiment, perhaps, but true nevertheless. As Boutros Boutros-Ghali wrote in 1996: '[T]he process of democratisation ... in order to take root and flourish, must derive from society itself ... . [I]t is essential that each State itself decide the form, pace and character of its democratization process'.[29]

The allure of Europe – the prospect of membership in the various European organisations – may help to tip the balance in favour of moderate forces in Bosnia and Kosovo, as it has among EU and NATO aspirants elsewhere. For instance, it was only when NATO made the resolution of long-standing border and minority issues between Hungary and Romania a condition for their membership of the organisation that protracted negotiations between the two countries were concluded and a basic treaty signed.[30] In East Timor, on the other hand, recent history, notably the trauma of violent polarisation, may help to guard against illiberal tendencies. And, to the extent that economic development contributes to social peace, democracy may also get a boost from the economic gains East Timor hopes to derive from exploitation of the oil and gas reserves off of its southern shores, starting in 2004 – provided those gains are distributed equitably.[31]

The limitations of rule by decree do not suggest that international authorities should be indifferent to political outcomes, only that they should not attempt to dictate them. Rather than pick winners, for instance, and risk a backlash as a result, they should instead endeavour – through the use of various incentives and sanctions – to create conditions conducive to the emergence of more liberal political tendencies. However, if institutions are utterly deficient and yet vital to the functioning of a state (as are courts, banks, etc.), it may be necessary to assume control of them, although this is more easily accomplished at the outset of an operation. There is a place for heavy-handedness, for instance, in the removal of individuals implicated in serious crimes and the obstruction of legal processes, but serial dismissals and bans on political parties that offend Western consciences yet reflect indigenous dispositions have not proved to be effective.[32]

Accountability

International administrations, like protectorates and trusteeships before them, derive their legitimacy in part from the notion of trust.[33] The idea of international rule over a foreign territory can be legitimate only if that rule is exercised on behalf of, and for the benefit of, the foreign population. To establish international administration on any other basis *primarily* would constitute exploitation. (One cannot ignore that some benefits – prestige, influence, etc. – may also accrue to the trustee.) Trust, in turn, is assured through the principle of accountability: the idea that a trustee must be responsible for its actions. But to whom is a transitional authority accountable?

Strictly speaking, a transitional administrator is accountable to the body that appoints him or her, whether that be the United Nations, in the cases of Eastern Slavonia, Kosovo and East Timor, or (additionally) the Peace Implementation Council, in the case of Bosnia.[34] Transitional administrators, and their staff, serve at the pleasure of these bodies, and it is to them that TAs report and are answerable. While local parties may also have to account to international bodies – for monies loaned or granted by international financial institutions, for instance – those bodies are not themselves accountable to the local population in any direct way. The World Bank answers to its Board of Governors (the 'shareholders'), not to the recipients of its funds (the 'stakeholders') – although representatives of the affected population may be consulted in the design of projects, and sundry mechanisms (for instance, the Bank's Inspection Panel) have been established to hear local complaints.[35] In addition, an ombudsman's office exists in both Kosovo and East Timor to hear complaints against all officials, international as well as local, but its jurisdiction is limited essentially to abuses of authority in relation to human rights.[36] Kosovo's Ombudsperson himself has criticised the virtual impunity with which UNMIK (and KFOR) operate, in view of the fact that UNMIK is not an ordinary peacekeeping operation but a surrogate state:

> With regard to UNMIK's exercise of its executive and legislative powers for the purpose of granting itself and its security counterpart immunity, the Ombudsperson recalls that the fundamental precept of the rule of law is that the executive and legislative authorities are bound by law and are not above it. He further recalls that, therefore, the actions and operations of these two branches of government must be subject to the oversight of the judiciary, as the arbiter of

legality in a democratic society. Finally, he recalls that these precepts govern the relationship between the state and the individual, who is the subject and not the object of the law. UNMIK Regulation 2000/47 [on the status, privileges and immunities of KFOR and UNMIK and their personnel] contravenes all of these principles.[37]

Limited accountability does not, however, mean the total absence of mechanisms for local scrutiny. In East Timor, the Cabinet, until its replacement by the Council of Ministers in September 2001, had the authority to call upon officials of the East Timor Transitional Administration (ETTA), the nascent government, to provide 'necessary and pertinent information', and the National Council could request Cabinet members to appear before it.[38] In addition, the Inspector General has a mandate to investigate any activities of the ETTA.[39] However, the ETTA (now the East Timor Public Administration) is an institution distinct from UNTAET, despite overlapping functions and shared personnel in the transitional period, and UNTAET is not subject to the same degree of local scrutiny. Rather, UNTAET is accountable principally to the United Nations.

One way in which the issue of accountability manifests itself is in the lack of transparency. From the standpoint of the affected population, the process of international decision-making can seem opaque, notwithstanding laudable efforts by the international authorities to communicate via the publication of various newsletters, reports and press releases, and the convening of public meetings. Sometimes the simple fact that relevant documents are not always available in local languages creates a barrier to comprehension. Or key decisions may be taken without sufficient insight being provided into the reasoning behind them, creating the impression of arbitrary rule. In relation to Bosnia, the International Crisis Group, in a 1996 report, made the following point:

Respect for Bosnian authorities and basic notions of reciprocity argue for at least the degree of transparency necessary for the Bosnian authorities and people to understand the basis for decisions, and the decision-making processes, that

> *so affect them. If the point of the international encampment in Bosnia is to 'teach' democracy, tolerance and good governance to the Bosnians then there is no better way to start than by example.*[40]

International and local non-governmental organisations (NGOs) may mitigate some of these deficiencies, providing vital information and critical analysis about the operations of a transitional administration and the conditions to which the administration is responding. They can also serve as fora for debating international policies within domestic politics.[41] Yet NGOs, too, are not always accountable to the local population (nor, for that matter, to national governments) for their actions.[42] Moreover, they often employ differing criteria in their evaluations, not all of which may be apparent or commensurate with that of other agencies.[43]

Lack of formal accountability to the affected population can inhibit efforts to build local capacity. In East Timor, despite the Transitional Administrator's clear commitment to the promotion of self-government, international staff initially balked at the idea of working under East Timorese officials when the latter were appointed to Cabinet and departmental posts.[44] Many of these staff maintained that, as they were employed by the United Nations, they were accountable to the UN and could not take direction from non-UN officials. Vieira de Mello was able to defuse the issue only by drawing attention to the fact that he was the Head of Mission, who has final authority, and was a Special Representative of the UN Secretary-General – though this reinforced perceptions that the transitional administration operates in the service of the United Nations rather than on behalf of the local population.

Exit Strategies

How is the transfer of power to the local population to be regulated and the exit of the international authorities achieved? To date there has been little experience with the termination of international administrations. Only UNTAES in Eastern Slavonia and UNTAC in Cambodia, a supervisory operation, have ended. Several relevant lessons can be drawn from this limited experience, however.

The first is that, while they are important for facilitating the transfer of authority from international to local actors and establishing the legitimacy of local rule, elections should not be regarded as the focal point of international involvement, as they were in Cambodia.[45] Even where international organisations are able to create the conditions that allow free and fair elections to be conducted (and the UN and the OSCE, in particular, now have considerable experience in this area), elections may not necessarily promote national reconciliation – rather, they can be extremely divisive, especially for territories where rival identity groups vie for political control. Indeed, in strongly divided societies it may be important for international authorities to avoid electoral systems that favour one group disproportionately, as 'first past the post' arrangements do. Proportional representation may be fairer, although it can lead to the chronic instability characteristic of governments lacking strong majorities[46]– and fairness may not always be the issue: a group may simply wish to be in possession of power at almost any cost. Another possibility was tried in Eastern Slavonia, where, to avoid polarisation, a power-sharing arrangement was negotiated between the ruling Croatian party and the leading Serb party, which made the election results more acceptable to Croats and Serbs alike.[47]

In their efforts to accommodate ethnic and political differences, interim administrations have tended to concentrate less on elections than on developing institutional safeguards for minority populations that, it is hoped, will endure beyond the transitional period. In East Timor, the Transitional Administrator has endeavoured to achieve this in part through the creation of inclusive institutions. From the start, he has sought to ensure broad representation on consultative bodies, appointing to the National Consultative Council three representatives from political parties that opposed independence for East Timor, among representatives of other groups; similar provisions have been made for the NCC's successor body, the National Council. These and other efforts to achieve accommodation between pro-independence and pro-autonomy groups have enjoyed broad support among a local leadership and general population inclined towards reconciliation. As a result, these institutional arrangements, or at least the spirit that animates them, are likely to survive the departure of the international authorities.

In Kosovo, comparable efforts have been made to achieve inclusiveness and, further, to guarantee multi-ethnicity, though they have been less successful because of highly polarised ethnic relations, between Albanians and Serbs especially. As in East Timor, the Transitional Administrator has sought to ensure broad representation by appointing Serb and other minority representatives to the Kosovo Transitional Council, the highest consultative body. Some Serbs, however, were unwilling initially to participate in the Council and others would do so only as observers. The change of regime in Belgrade has helped to foster a more constructive attitude among Kosovo Serbs, evident in their willingness to take part in Kosovo's November 2001 Assembly elections.[48] This serves to illustrate, once again, the impact that regional dynamics can have on international efforts to administer war-torn territories, although efforts to achieve full participation by Kosovo Serbs in the interim administration have been largely unsuccessful.

In the case of Kosovo, the international efforts have also focused on the design of constitutional measures that aim to empower and protect Kosovo's beleaguered minority groups. The *Constitutional Framework for Provisional Self-Government*, promulgated by the Transitional Administrator on 15 May 2001,[49] reserves 10 seats for Kosovo Serbs in the newly created 120-seat Assembly and 10 seats for other minority groups.[50] Two ministerial posts are also reserved for representatives of the Kosovo Serbs and another minority group. Moreover, minorities have the right to challenge any proposed legislation that threatens their 'vital interests' – a procedure, however, that avoids the pitfalls of a similar provision available to Bosnia's constituent peoples.[51] The *Constitutional Framework* also establishes extensive rights for minorities, allowing them to use their language and script freely before courts, agencies and all other public bodies; to receive education in their own language; to enjoy access to information in their own language; to establish associations to promote the interests of their community; to establish their own media and to be guaranteed access to public broadcast outlets as well as programming in relevant languages.[52] A number of these same rights, it is interesting to note, are denied to minorities in many of the European states that are promoting respect for them so vigorously in Kosovo.

The second lesson that can be drawn from experience to date with the termination of international administrations is the importance of a phased exit strategy, the pace of devolution being commensurate with the demonstrated ability of the local leadership to meet specified benchmarks – the protection of minority populations high among them. Such an approach was employed with some success by UNTAES, although the mission was constrained by a fixed two-year limit on its mandate. In the first phase of the exit strategy, the Transitional Administrator devolved responsibility to Croatia for the major part of the civil administration, maintaining the authority to intervene and, critically, to overrule decisions if necessary. The devolution of remaining executive functions was subject to satisfactory performance on the part of the Croatian government, notwithstanding Zagreb's failure to meet all its obligations, notably the resolution of key legal issues regarding Croatian property, amnesty and citizenship laws, which discriminated against Serbs.[53] (The UN, in response, delayed its transfer of authority to Zagreb; it could not, however, maintain control indefinitely.[54]) Kosovo and East Timor have also been conceived as multi-phased missions, yet, unlike UNTAES, they are not subject to fixed time constraints.

A third lesson is the importance of effective follow-on arrangements. This is a role for which regional organisations may be well suited. In Eastern Slavonia UNTAES was succeeded by a support group of 180 civilian UN police monitors and an OSCE mission that has been responsible for monitoring implementation of the agreements that the government of Croatia signed with UNTAES.[55] The OSCE worked closely with UNTAES before the start of its mission, thus allowing it to become familiar with the principal issues, and its mission has reported regularly to governments on Croatia's progress towards meeting its international commitments. Governments, in turn, have been able to use the information to pressure Croatia to comply with its obligations. However, what progress has been made in the case of Croatia – admittedly limited in areas that directly affect the return and reintegration of Croatian Serbs – owes as much (if not more) to the collapse of the Tudjman regime and the establishment of a successor government more interested in international and regional cooperation as it does to third-party pressure.[56]

Indeed this observation points to a further lesson: the value of incentives (in this case the prospect of membership of the various European organisations) when and where they are available. We have already noted the 'tipping effect' that the possibility of entry into Europe may have for the Balkan countries, although obviously this is not a goal to which all territories can aspire. Assistance in financing local initiatives that contribute to improved relations between ethnic and other groups may also make a difference. It is arguable that external support for an Albanian-language university in Macedonia, among other assistance, might have inhibited the violence that erupted there in the spring of 2001.

In the end, of course, it is the local authorities who bear primary responsibility for the policies that prevail. Where these authorities are determined to pursue divisive and even fratricidal policies, international and regional organisations may need to contemplate indefinite 'occupation' to contain these tendencies. But in some cases disengagement also deserves consideration, bearing in mind that ultimately there may be limits to what outside parties can do to promote the values that underpin a democratic and tolerant society.[57]

Chapter 4

Enhancing International Administration

Since the end of the Cold War, the United Nations' and other organisations' assumption of increased responsibility for conflict management (including, but not limited to, the administration of war-torn territories) has spawned a vast literature concerned with ways of strengthening international and regional capabilities to meet these new challenges. The UN has itself contributed significantly to the debate, most notably with the report of the Panel on United Nations Peace Operations (better known as the Brahimi report) published on 21 August 2000.[1] The report, in turn, has been the basis for potentially far-reaching reforms that the UN Secretariat, with the support of some member states, has begun to introduce subsequently, although it remains to be seen how much of the reform agenda will actually be implemented. At a regional level, too, institutional changes have been taking place that may allow the European Union, in particular, to respond more effectively to the challenges of conflict management in its own backyard and perhaps farther afield. Measures are also being pursued by individual national governments to redress institutional and other deficiencies in this area.

There is no dearth, then, of imaginative, indeed practical, proposals and initiatives for the enhancement of peace operations, and while the Brahimi report – the centrepiece of the current debate – deals only briefly with the challenges specific to international administration,[2] much of its analysis and many of its recommendations have broad relevance to the subject. Other ideas, more in keeping with secular trends that favour greater reliance on the private sector, deserve consideration too. This final section will take stock of recent policy initiatives that promise to enhance the capacity of international administration, identify deficiencies likely to remain, and suggest steps that could be taken to remedy them. Weaknesses in three key areas – planning and management of operations, rapid deployment of assets (particularly in relation to providing internal security), and the 'politics' of international administrations – account for some of the more serious shortcomings associated with these initiatives. There are other issues that affect international and regional organisations' capability for carrying out operations of this nature, but overcoming weaknesses in these three areas in particular would contribute significantly to enhancing the effectiveness of international administration.

Planning and Management of Operations

Among the principal international actors concerned, only the United Nations and its associated agencies have established structures and procedures that lend themselves readily to administering war-torn territories; all the others rely on *ad hoc* arrangements – reflected, for example, in the set-up of the Office of the (PIC-appointed) High Representative. Nevertheless the UN, we have seen, has experienced numerous difficulties in planning and managing these operations. The Organisation is seldom prepared for the worst, missions are planned hurriedly, and support for them is insufficient long after their initial deployment. These difficulties arise in part from resource constraints, organisational structural impediments and procedural inflexibility. Many of these areas – chronic problems for the UN – have been the targets of renewed reform efforts recently by the UN Secretariat.

Inadequate resources, particularly within the Department of Peacekeeping Operations, have contributed significantly to the litany of problems described in this study. At the time the Brahimi panel released its report, expenditures for DPKO staffing and related costs for planning and maintaining all peacekeeping operations were projected to be a mere two percent of these operations' total cost. The report observed, 'A management analyst familiar with the operational requirements of large organizations, public or private, that operate substantial field-deployed elements might well conclude that an organization trying to run a field-oriented enterprise on two per cent central support costs was undersupporting its field people and very likely burning out its support structures in the process'.[3] As a result, the panel recommended a substantial increase in resources for central support of peacekeeping operations which the General Assembly approved in December 2000, leading to the establishment of 93 additional posts in DPKO.[4] In October 2001 the GA's Advisory Committee on Administrative and Budgetary Questions agreed to the establishment of a further 92 posts for DPKO. Together, these new posts represent a 50 percent increase over pre-Brahimi staffing levels.[5]

Adjusting staffing levels alone, of course, will not provide the UN with the capacity for more effective planning: a fundamental shift in thinking within the organisation is required as well. Just as military alliances and many state ministries draw up contingency plans – as NATO did in anticipation of its involvement in Bosnia and Kosovo – so planning for actual or prospective crises where the UN may be expected to play an active role should also be made obligatory for DPKO, DPA, OCHA and other UN agencies.[6] The UN might even be able to engage the services of private think tanks to assist in the formulation of such plans. These plans would need to be updated periodically in response to changing circumstances.

The European Union now has machinery that could, with significant expansion, also allow it to conduct planning of this kind.[7] In October 1999 its Policy Planning and Early Warning Unit (PPEWU) was established, as called for by the Amsterdam Treaty.[8] The PPEWU, which comprises diplomats drawn from the EU member states, officials from the Council Secretariat and one military officer with WEU/NATO experience, drafts position papers and 'think pieces' for the High Representative for Common Foreign and Security Policy, currently Javier Solana. Its work is complemented, and to some degree perhaps duplicated, by the European Union Military Staff Organisation (EUMS), whose establishment the European Council approved at its Nice summit in December 2000.[9] The EUMS performs early warning, situation assessment and strategic planning for the so-called Petersberg tasks: humanitarian and rescue tasks, peacekeeping tasks, and combat-force tasks in crisis management, including 'peacemaking' (i.e. peace enforcement).[10] An institutional basis for contingency planning thus exists within both the UN and the EU, provided that member states are prepared to use these institutions for that purpose.

Moreover, the UN has recently introduced a number of structural changes that could strengthen its capacity to plan and maintain complex operations. Although modest, measures to improve communication between DPKO and DPA – including the establishment of an interdepartmental working group (on the Balkans) and the decision to co-locate the departments' respective regional divisions – are likely to enhance information-sharing.[11] DPKO and DPA remain fiercely protective of their respective territories, however, and a more sensible measure would be to merge the two into a single department – but the UN Secretariat has long resisted such a recommendation.

Much more important for co-ordination and collaboration has been the Secretariat's commitment to establishing Integrated Mission Task Forces (IMTFs) that will bring together personnel from the many relevant departments, agencies, funds and programmes to plan and manage complex operations under the authority of a single co-ordinator, who will report either to the Under-Secretary-General for Peacekeeping Operations or to the Under-Secretary-General for Political Affairs, depending on the nature of the operation.[12] The IMTF team will normally comprise at its core one or two political officers involved from the start in pre-mission negotiations, one representative each from the humanitarian and development fields with specific field knowledge of the mission area, one military and/or civilian police officer, and one representative from the administrative and logistics support area.[13] A modified version of the IMTF mechanism was established in March 2001 to plan for the post-UNTAET international follow-up presence in East Timor, and another is in place for Afghanistan.[14] The question is whether IMTFs will have sufficient executive authority to be able to harmonise UN agency participation.

There can be no template for an operation as complex as a transitional administration; however, 'best practices' and 'errors' can be distilled from past experiences, and efforts can be made to disseminate this knowledge within organisations and to develop standard operating procedures on the basis of them. The idea of distillation reflects the thinking that underlay the establishment in April 1995 of the Lessons Learned Unit within DPKO, now called the Peacekeeping Best Practices Unit. But the unit has never been very effective. Its studies remain largely unread, or even un-published (in the case of UNPROFOR), with staff having little time or inclination to consider them, as they do not seem pertinent to the specific operational requirements of current or future missions.[15] The Secretary-General has proposed the creation of a new unit, a Peacekeeping Strategic Planning Unit,[16] represent-atives of which would serve on IMTFs, but it is not at all evident that this body will enhance the capacity of IMTFs. It would be better if the unit were also to have the authority to examine and offer comment on all relevant planning and oper-ational documents in much the same way that the accounting division of large organisations scrutinises proposed financial expenditures.

To develop standard operating procedures on the basis of challenges as diverse and complex as those of international admin-istrations may seem an impossible and even misguided task, but certain structural and procedural characteristics are already being replicated informally. For instance, the design and function of consultative mechanisms adopted first by UNMIK and then by UNTAET are very similar. And the profile of civilian specialists used for operations of this kind is in many respects the same – allowance being made for unusual requirements, such as East Timor's particular need for land administration experts. The ques-tion is whether these experiences provide a model for future operations. To the extent that they do, they can serve to facilitate rapid deployment of a mission, the absence of which has been one of the principal weaknesses of international administration. Stan-dard operating procedures already exist for military and humani-tarian operations; there is no reason why they could not also be developed for some of the other aspects of transitional admin-istrations.

Rapid and Effective Deployment

The rapid and effective deployment of human resources and materiel to a distressed region is vital to the success of any peace operation, but it is particularly important for the international administration of war-torn territories. The sheer scope of the operation means that there is more chance for failure (or at least the *perception* of failure), because there are many more fronts on which transitional authorities must operate. Moreover, many of these areas are closely inter-related. Without adequate detention centres and the personnel to administer them, for instance, police and judicial efforts to maintain law and order will be seriously compromised – as they were in Kosovo, where limited detention facilities in the early days resulted in the release of convicted criminals to make room for 'harder' criminals.[17] Also, the leverage of international officials is at its height in the early phase of a mission, and the credibility that may be lost as a consequence of the slow and inefficient deployment of resources is often difficult to regain.

International administrations require the rapid deployment of military personnel, civilian police, civilian specialists and large stocks of equipment. Yet the UN Standby Arrangements System (UNSAS), by which governments agree to make military assets available to the UN at seven, 15, 30, 60 or 90 days' notice, and the pre-positioning of essential equipment at the UN Logistics Base at Brindisi, Italy, are not sufficient to ensure an effective response to the requirements of future operations of this kind. The requirements of international administrations can easily dwarf available supplies, and UNSAS arrangements do not bind governments to provide troops for a given operation. Indeed, it is only because of the urgency attached to the three Balkan operations by NATO and to East Timor by Australia that it was possible to achieve a rapid deployment of troops in those cases. With respect to the rapid deployment of civilian police and civilian specialists, the UN and regional organisations are even less well prepared.

The UN is taking several steps to improve the current situation, as are member states, jointly and singly. As suggested by Brahimi, the Secretary-General is seeking to draw up an on-call list of approximately 100 experienced, well-qualified military officers who will be available for deployment on seven days' notice – first to New York, for mission guidance, and then to the field, where they will constitute the nucleus of the mission's headquarters.[18] Personnel selected for inclusion in this core group would be pre-qualified, pre-trained and prepared to serve for a period of up to two years. So far, the Secretary-General has communicated the profiles of expertise required, and he is now canvassing member states to nominate officers. Yet, even if he succeeds in establishing a reliable on-call list (similar efforts have failed in the past), a core group of 100 will hardly be able to establish and maintain security in a war-torn territory; and the goal of 90 days for full deployment of a complex peace operation, which Brahimi recommended and the Secretary-General has endorsed, will be extremely difficult to meet.[19] In the absence of a UN standing army or police force, a more rapid and effective response may not be realistic; hence consideration should perhaps be given to greater use of 'lead nations' or 'coalitions of the willing' for this purpose, although this might mean some loss of UN oversight and control.

It is the challenge of policing that transitional authorities have been least well equipped to meet, and this is one area where future demand is likely to be great, even if the number of international administrations does not increase. We can expect continued incidence of intra-state conflict across the globe; deploying police officers to war-torn societies in response to this will be much less controversial for national governments, and in many ways more appropriate, than deploying soldiers.

The inadequate supply of police officers to serve in international operations, and the fact that many of them may be poorly qualified, mean that special measures must be adopted to enlarge the pool of available candidates and to enhance the standard overall. Brahimi has recommended that states establish national pools of active police officers, supplemented if necessary by capable retired officers, who would be trained to a common (UN) standard and who could be made available in the context of the UN's standby arrangements. As with military officers, Brahimi has also suggested the creation of an on-call list of 100 police officers ready to be deployed at seven days' notice.[20] To that end, the UN Secretary-General has defined the profiles of necessary expertise, as well as the associated logistical and other support requirements (e.g., forensic experts and labs), for a phased deployment within 90 days.[21] DPKO has also developed 'Principles and Guidelines for United Nations Civilian Police Operations' in an effort to establish common standards and operation procedures.[22] Finally, to enhance the cohesion of the different police components within an operation, Brahimi has recommended the establishment of joint training exercises.[23] With this in mind, Britain has initiated training programmes in seven regions around the world – in Latin America, Africa and Asia – involving up to 10 countries in each case.[24]

Even before the release of the Brahimi report, the EU had undertaken to enhance its capacity to provide police officers for international peace operations, including post-conflict international administrations. At a meeting of the European Council at Santa Maria da Feira on 19 and 20 June 2000, EU member states agreed to establish, by 2003, the capacity to provide 5,000 police officers to international missions across a range of crisis-prevention and crisis-management operations, from advising, training and monitoring local police up to executive policing. As many as 1,000 of these officers would be available within 30 days.[25] These forces are to be 'robust', integrated and interoperable units, which can be deployed in response to a request from an international or regional organisation, notably the UN or the OSCE, or as an autonomous EU police operation. In May 2001 Javier Solana announced that the EU 'seem[s] to have reached' its goal for rapid deployment.[26] By that time some 3,500 EU police officers were already serving in international missions, 3,100 of them in the Balkans. The United States, too, has sought to enhance its contribution to civilian policing internationally. Presidential Decision Directive (PDD) 71, promulgated by President Clinton on 24 February 2000, directs the State Department to establish a $10-million programme to pre-screen and train an estimated 2,000 US police officers for participation in international missions – some two-and-a-half times the number of US police officers currently serving abroad.[27] The 2,000 would constitute a pool from which to draw, and to rotate, police officers. While the fate of the directive under President Bush is uncertain, the administration appears to be moving forward hesitantly with the initiative, funding for which Congress had already approved. Adequate training is sorely needed: US reliance on a private company – DynCorp Technical Services – to recruit police to serve in international missions has led in the past to the deployment of highly unqualified personnel (although US officers are generally far from the weakest in any mission).[28]

The EU's proposed deployment of up to 1,000 police officers within 30 days, while indeed rapid, may, however, be too slow to prevent the emergence of a security vacuum in a crisis area. Hence, where they may be deployed before police officers (as in Kosovo and East Timor) or alongside them, international military forces must be trained and willing to assume greater law-enforcement responsibilities. Allied soldiers readily accepted such a role in Germany after the Second World War; a special Constabulary force of 30,000 US soldiers, distinguished by their bright yellow scarves and special uniforms, was established in January 1946 to carry out policing and riot control – a task they performed without hesitation.[29] More recently, the US State Department White Paper on PDD 71 acknowledged the need for US soldiers to conduct law-enforcement activities in peace operations for a limited period of time until civilian organisations are able to assume responsibility for these tasks.[30] For those military forces that have specific civilian police experience – the Italian Carabinieri, the Spanish Guardia Civil and the French Gendarmerie – the challenge is by no means an alien one. The use of military personnel for this purpose underscores the importance of developing an interim legal code that all soldiers can employ pending the establishment of local rule of law. It is also worth considering compulsory language training for all international personnel (military or civilian) who perform police duties, in light of the close engagement they can expect to have with the local community. Kenyan forces underwent language training in Tetum before their deployment to East Timor, and this earned them considerable respect among the residents.

The rapid deployment of civilian specialists and materiel, unlike the other categories of resources, is hampered especially by cumbersome procedures relating to the recruitment of personnel and the procurement of goods. In the case of the United Nations, decisions on hiring and firing staff and disbursing funds are, for the most part, centralised in New York. But the scale of operations as large as UNMIK or UNTAET, and the many critical areas requiring prompt attention as a result, mean that international administrations suffer more than other peace operations as a consequence of these practices: 'It is like being asked to perform Olympic gymnastics and then being placed in a straitjacket', Vieira de Mello has observed.[31] As regards goods, it can take anywhere from 17 to 27 weeks to procure vital equipment such as communications equipment, generators, heavy vehicles, office furniture and prefabricated buildings.[32] And as far as recruitment goes, DPKO recruitment officers have many more applications to process than any other UN agency (more than 2,600 applications each a year, as against the average of 761 for other departments[33]) – indeed, 11 months after the UN Security Council voted to establish UNTAET, the mission was still not fully staffed.[34] These kinds of problems have plagued UN peacekeeping operations for years.

There is the further related problem that rules regarding personnel recruitment and the use of funds and assets are too restrictive for the operational requirements of an international administration. For instance, the UN and other multilateral organisations – concerned to achieve geographic balance – will often avoid hiring many staff from a single country where the relevant expertise is available (sometimes *gratis*), even though delays or spectacularly poor appointments may result. And, while strict regulations on the use of funds and assets make good sense in terms of central managerial oversight, they deny transitional authorities the flexibility they need to be able to respond effectively to conditions on the ground. (Again, given the complex and dynamic nature of the situation, this can be more problematic for international administrations than for other peace operations.) The local population, moreover, is generally not able to comprehend the failure of their 'trustees' to expend allocated funds promptly to deal with obvious and urgent needs and may grow resentful in the face of apparent indifference.

Some measures are being taken to address these related problems. The Secretary-General has recommended (and the General Assembly seems likely to accept) an enhancement of the UN Logistics Base at Brindisi to allow the pre-purchase and maintenance of the most critical items needed for rapid deployment within 30 days (for peacekeeping operations) and 90 days (for complex peacekeeping operations). Remaining items would be purchased on an *ad hoc* basis using pre-mandate commitment authority and retainer and no-fee contracts with designated suppliers. It was pre-purchased goods and services that made possible the relatively quick deployment of the UN Mission in Ethiopia and Eritrea (UNMEE) in September 2000 – this was an accident of fate, however, because the goods and services had been acquired for another mission (to the Democratic Republic of the Congo) that was delayed.[35]

With respect to personnel, Brahimi suggested establishing a roster of civilian specialists in a variety of skill areas who, having indicated that they would be available on short notice, would be vetted, interviewed, medically cleared and provided with the basic orientation applicable to field service – all in advance.[36] The UN has since begun to establish an internet system known as the Galaxy Project, which, when completed, will allow the Office of Human Resources Management to receive applications online, screen them on the basis of established criteria and automatically rank candidates in accordance with job requirements (the system will also enable applicants to update their personal histories and availability periodically).[37] Further enhancements of the Galaxy Project should make it possible to create a roster system along the lines suggested by the Brahimi report. Another way to eliminate the deficiencies of the present system would be to entrust individual states with responsibility for whole sectors of administration – a variation on the 'lead nation' concept. Some members of the East Timorese leadership, notably those who lived in exile in Australia, have indicated that they would have been happy to have had Australia train the territory's civil servants.[38] As with standby military and police officers, producing a roster of civilian specialists requires identification of the different occupational groups that an international administration tends to need and definition of the associated skill requirements.

Greater delegation of authority to the field is also needed to enhance the effectiveness of international administrations, although central oversight of operations needs to be maintained. The UN has already experimented successfully with relocating recruitment personnel from New York to Kosovo, thus reducing hiring delays and vacancy rates and also allowing field administrators more input into the recruitment process. And transitional administrators need greater flexibility in managing their budgets. UN rules make it difficult for a mission to expend resources on anything other than the mission itself. This may not be problematic for most peace-support operations, but it would be helpful for an operation whose purpose is to facilitate the emergence of a new state, or at least to promote substantial autonomy, to permit the use of UN resources – buildings, computers, vehicles – by fledgling indigenous institutions. UNTAET had over 500 vehicles for use by its own staff, but UN regulations, had they been strictly observed, would have prevented any of them being made available to East Timor's senior political leaders.[39] UN procurement rules should also be revised to allow transitional administrators greater authority to buy goods and services directly, rather than through New York. (The current ceiling on local acquisition is $200,000 per purchase order.) Often goods and services are both available locally. The Brahimi report calls for enhanced field authority, but the Field Administration and Logistics Division of DPKO (tasked with exploring this and related proposals aimed at enabling rapid and effective mission deployment) has so far been unable to assess the different options – owing, tellingly, to staffing shortfalls. Yet there is no reason why the UN cannot follow the example of the World Bank, which oversees billions of dollars of procurement locally by national governments and their agencies each year.

Political Factors

Conflating international administrations with complex peace operations tends to obscure some of the fundamental political issues at the core of these state-building initiatives. These issues need to be acknowledged and, in some cases, addressed more directly if transitional administrators are to be able to make better informed and more legitimate choices concerning the post-conflict reconstruction and development of a territory.

No international administration can function without having a political vision, implied or stated, for the society it is administering. Yet how does a transitional administrator give concrete expression to such notions as 'democratic development', 'multiethnic society', 'peaceful coexistence' and 'political diversity', among the other various advertised mission objectives? (Bernard Kouchner is said to have read the text of UN Security Council Resolution 1244 twice every morning in a vain attempt to understand what was meant by the term 'substantial autonomy'.[40]) There are obviously many options available to transitional authorities within the broad confines of their mandates, and the ramifications of the choices they make are potentially far reaching.

Whose opinion should count in these matters? International transitional authorities cannot function as governments answerable *primarily* to the people whose territories they administer. International trusteeships are not representative democracies; they are institutions created and sustained by international processes, which, though themselves democratically deficient in certain respects,[41] establish a legitimate basis and the parameters for the exercise of international authority. Moreover, in the face of threats to the peace for which local authorities bear responsibility, or a humanitarian emergency that exceeds the capacity of the local population to cope, one can justify a partial or complete suspension of sovereignty, at least temporarily. Notwithstanding these considerations, greater effort needs to be made to ensure a meaningful degree of accountability to the local population, otherwise an operation will suffer from a deficit of legitimacy.

Consultation with representatives of the local community is already a priority for most transitional authorities. (UNMIK established the Kosovo Transitional Council within a week of the mission's start,[42] and it was UNTAET's second regulation that set up a National Consultative Council.) The question arises, however, whom should a transitional authority choose to consult? Sergio Vieira de Mello established close ties with CNRT and its President, Xanana Gusmão, in particular, undoubtedly reinforcing Gusmão's power and leading some observers to argue that the UN was prejudicing the political process.[43] Indeed it was, as UN officials admit – CNRT and Gusmão were considered to be interlocutors who could be counted on to work with the UN in support of its aims, and UNTAET thus felt comfortable attributing a predominant partnership role to CNRT, which, moreover, enjoyed very broad popular support. In Kosovo the situation was different.

There the UN's main interlocutor initially was Hashim Thaci, the leader of the Kosovo Liberation Army (KLA), who is committed to achieving independence for Kosovo through violent means if necessary. The UN had little choice but to deal with Thaci, given the KLA's power, but it sought to dilute his influence and to temporise, in the hope that Ibrahim Rugova (the more moderate 'President' of Kosovo, then in Rome) would return to the province and draw support away from his radical rival.[44] These may be prudent and necessary calculations for an enterprise as inescapably political as an international administration, but they risk putting international officials in the awkward position of choosing sides, and thus alienating elements of the population. On the other hand, to say 'let the process decide' begs the question of which processes to adopt – because institutional design (e.g. electoral procedures) often has significant implications for political outcomes.[45]

These are not matters which the local population can always decide. There are, though, other mechanisms that can strengthen accountability. One is enlarging the institution of the ombudsman. Complaints against any official, local or international, can be filed with Kosovo's and East Timor's ombudsmen, but these officials are concerned principally with the protection of human rights. However the ombudsman could also be empowered to receive and investigate complaints from citizens about the process of international administration – for instance, procedural improprieties, bias or the lack of due process – and make recommendations to the transitional authority on the basis of his or her findings.[46] The ombudsman should not be able to strike down legislation, but the recommendations would be likely to carry weight.

A second mechanism for strengthening accountability is expanded jurisdiction for the local high courts. As these courts demonstrate that they are capable of deciding issues in a fair and impartial manner, they might be given authority to review the transitional authority's exercise of powers if and when these seem to be incompatible with locally enacted legislation. The Constitutional Court of Bosnia, for instance, has jurisdiction over issues concerning whether a law is compatible with the constitution, international human-rights law and general rules of public international law.[47] In November 2000, for the first time, the court reviewed a decision of the High Representative (the creation of a unified border service for Bosnia), which – though the legislation was found to be in conformity with the constitution – established a precedent for a local institution challenging the legality of an international act.[48] Before local institutions can assume more authority, however, it may be necessary to amend the international legislation defining the powers of the transitional administrator.

Mindful of the weaknesses, some serious, that have arisen in the context of the international administration of war-torn territories and 'peace operations' generally, the UN, other international organisations and national governments have pledged to renew their efforts at institutional reform. There is no *a priori* reason for supposing that the proposals identified above cannot be implemented, and the Brahimi report, among other high-profile exercises in self-criticism, may indeed generate meaningful support for change. Pending such change, the scope for the effective management of complex emergencies of the kind explored on these pages will remain unnecessarily limited.

Conclusion

The international administrations of Eastern Slavonia, Bosnia, Kosovo and East Timor represent some of the boldest experiments in the management and settlement of intra-state conflict ever attempted by the United Nations and other third parties. In each case these bodies have assumed responsibility for the governance of territories to a degree unprecedented in recent history. This study has sought to assess the effectiveness of international transitional administrations and to explore the key issues that arise in the context of these experiences. Although it may be too early to pass final judgement on them (except for UNTAES, these initiatives represent 'works in progress'), some partial conclusions can nevertheless be drawn.

The experiences examined here suggest that several factors enhance the likelihood of success of an operation of this nature – if success is defined broadly in terms of significant progress towards eliminating the threat of violent conflict, achieving a political settlement and establishing viable state or territorial institutions. The first of these is *favourable objective conditions*. Where parties to a conflict either face or have suffered a decisive military defeat, they will have fewer opportunities to resist the authority of an international administration, and may even welcome it as their best hope of securing some measure of protection and representation in a successor regime. The prospect of defeat by the Croatian Army no doubt induced the Croatian Serbs to work with international authorities in Eastern Slavonia, however begrudgingly, just as actual defeat had done in the cases of Nazi Germany and Imperial Japan.[1] By contrast, the absence of a decisive military victory by any of the warring parties in Bosnia constrained those who were formulating treaty terms that all parties would accept, rendering it difficult to establish viable state institutions – a problem that plagues the High Representative to this day.[2]

Third-party states are sometimes in a position to help mould the conditions under which international authorities will function as administrators: for instance, by allowing or even abetting one side to gain the strategic advantage in a conflict. They must be careful, however, to ensure that, when the fighting is over, the international authorities are equipped – and willing – to disarm and demobilise local armed forces as necessary, to guard against residual resistance. Otherwise international authorities may only be able to play a supervisory role at best.

The attitudes of regional powers make up a further component of objective conditions. If these powers seek to exploit the internal turmoil for their own advantage, international efforts at state-building process may be seriously undermined.[3] Without the support of China, the Soviet Union, Vietnam and the ASEAN states, for instance, UNTAC in Cambodia would have been unable to operate effectively at all.[4] Geography matters too. A small territory is often easier to administer than a large one, where it is more difficult to establish a secure environment unless international soldiers and police are deployed in very large numbers.

The second factor that may affect the ease or difficulty of administering a war-torn territory is the *clarity and appeal of operational aims*. Where the aims are well-defined and attract broad support among the local population, the administrative authority enjoys distinct advantages, as it has in East Timor. It may not always be possible to achieve a clarity of aims which all parties will support, however. When the local political elite, or third parties, or both, do not share a common vision for the future, it may be necessary to establish interim arrangements and defer a decision about the final outcome until a later date, in the hope that with time a mutually acceptable political settlement can be achieved. Of course, there is a risk that in the interim period local authorities will seek to create 'facts on the ground' in an effort to prejudice a determination about the final outcome – as has occurred with Albanian persecution of Kosovo Serbs. For this reason it is all the more important that international authorities are able to establish a safe and secure environment for all persons. The alternative to adopting interim measures – imposing a settlement – may alienate a significant portion of the population and create incentives for spoilers, although it must also be recognised that in some cases parties to a conflict may refuse to accept any settlement or interim measures that fall short of their goals.

A clear political endpoint does not necessarily mean a precise time frame, though. Indeed, too strict a timetable can work against achievement of an operation's objectives (arguably, this was the case in Eastern Slavonia). Rather than seek to establish a new *modus vivendi*, local parties may dig in their heels until the international authorities have departed, or they may make concessions but then fail to implement them. An international civil and military presence of indefinite duration may thus be necessary until a new and more conciliatory political elite emerges. If it does not, an international security force may suffice to keep the peace (as it has in Cyprus), although missions of long duration with dim prospects for a political settlement are unlikely to attract sustained international support. On the other hand, if third-party states choose to withdraw their support altogether they risk triggering renewed hostilities.

The *type of operation* also has implications for the ease or difficulty of administration. A supervisory operation – one that relies largely on the co-operation of the local parties for successful implementation of its mandate – is vulnerable to obstructionism if any of the parties chooses simply to reject the agenda of the international authorities. A transitional administration that has full executive authority is better equipped to meet this challenge. While it may not always be necessary for administrators to exercise full authority – and they should seek to devolve as much responsibility to the local population as feasible – without it, they are more likely to find local actors frustrating their efforts to achieve the aims of their mandates.

Finally, the *structure of the operation* – notably, the degree of authority (civil and military) invested in the transitional administrator, and the relationship between the administrator and the component organisations – also has considerable bearing on the success of an operation. Unified authority, strong co-ordination, and a willingness by headquarters to delegate responsibility to the field, all enhance a transitional authority's capacity to administer a war-torn territory effectively.

These are, however, not the only factors that contribute to the success of an international administration. The readiness of states and organisations to plan early and deploy sufficient resources rapidly also has enormous consequences for an operation. These requirements extend well beyond the framework of any single operation and point to the need for broader institutional reform. Ultimately, of course, it is for the local population and its leadership to decide whether to accept a peaceful accommodation of differences. A people determined to carry on its struggle may succeed in frustrating even the best of international designs.

International administration is the Rolls-Royce of conflict-management strategies, and it is doubtful that there will be the political will to repeat the experience very often. But, as the events of 11 September 2001 demonstrate, we live in a world where it is no longer possible to assume that weak or failed states are something the rest of the world can easily ignore. Robert Cooper employs the term 'pre-state, post-imperial chaos' to refer to regions of the world that, no longer strategically important to major powers, have succumbed to political disorder, desperate poverty and civil conflict. 'The existence of such a zone of chaos is nothing new; but previously such areas, precisely because of their chaos, were isolated from the rest of the world. Not so today.'[5] As a consequence of globalisation, these zones of chaos today are fertile ground for the establishment of drug, crime and terrorist syndicates from which no country may be immune – as the crisis of Afghanistan makes clear.[6] The international administration of war-torn territories may be costly and imperfect, but less interventionist measures, in some cases, are worse alternatives.

Notes

Introduction

1 Scholarly articles that foreshadowed this development include Gerald B. Helman and Steven R. Ratner, 'Saving Failed States', *Foreign Policy*, no. 89, Winter 1992–93, pp. 3–20, and Peter Lyon, 'The Rise and Fall and Possible Revival of International Trusteeship', *Journal of Commonwealth & Comparative Politics*, vol. 31, no. 1, March 1993, pp. 96–110.

2 Figures drawn from Stockholm International Peace Research Institute, *SIPRI Yearbook* (Oxford: Oxford University Press for SIPRI, 1989–2001). A major armed conflict is defined here as prolonged combat between the military forces of two or more governments or one government and at least one organised armed group, incurring battle-related deaths of at least 1,000 people.

3 *Humanitarian Intervention: Legal and Political Aspects* (Copenhagen: Danish Institute of International Affairs, 1999), pp. 88–93. 'Unilateral' is understood here to mean intervention without authorisation from the UN Security Council.

4 Transcript of briefing given by Blair to the Economic Club of Chicago, Hilton Hotel, Chicago, 22 April 1999. Text available at http://www.fco.gov.uk/news/speechtext.asp?2316.

5 Author interviews with UNTAET officials, Dili. As early as March 1999, the Australian Defence Force (ADF) moved an additional brigade of troops to Darwin and was readying other elements for a possible deployment on short notice. See James Cotton, 'Against the Grain: The East Timor Intervention', *Survival*, vol. 43, no. 1, Spring 2001, p. 131.

6 The Allied reconstruction of Germany and Japan after World War Two were similarly ambitious but, in contrast with today's international administrations, were undertaken principally by individual states, sometimes acting in concert.

7 These concerns are reflected in *Refashioning the Dialogue: Regional Perspectives on the Brahimi Report on UN Peace Operations* (New York: Center on International Co-operation and International Peace Academy, 2001).

Chapter 1

1 This categorisation draws on Jarat Chopra's work on peace maintenance. See, in particular, his *Peace-Maintenance: The Evolution of International Political Authority* (London: Routledge, 1999). Chopra employs the terms 'assistance', 'partnership', 'control' and 'governorship' to describe the range of authority (p. 16).

2 UN Security Council Resolution 745 (1992), adopted on 28 February 1992, established the mission.

3 *Agreement on a Comprehensive Political Settlement of the Cambodia Conflict*, 23 October 1991, Annex 1, Section B, para. 1, UN Document A/46/608-S/23177, 30 October 1991.

4 Janet E. Heininger, *Peacekeeping in Transition: The United Nations in Cambodia* (New York: Twentieth Century Fund Press, 1994), p. 6; and Mats Berdal and Michael Leifer, 'Cambodia', in James Mayall (ed.), *The New Interventionism 1991–1994: United Nations Experience in Cambodia, former Yugoslavia and Somalia* (Cambridge: Cambridge University Press, 1996), pp. 25–58.

5 UN Security Council Resolution 1037 (1996), adopted on 15 January 1996, established the mission.

6 On UNTEA see Rosalyn Higgins, *United Nations Peacekeeping, 1946–1967: Documents and Commentary* (Oxford: Oxford University Press for the Royal Institute of International Affairs, 1969–81), vol. 2 (Asia), pp. 101–6. See also Paul W. Van Der Veur, 'The United Nations in West Irian: A Critique', *International Organization*, vol. 18, no. 1, Winter 1964, pp. 53–73.

7 The *Basic Agreement on the Region of Eastern Slavonia, Baranja and Western Sirmium* (also known as the *Erdut Agreement*) was signed on 12 November 1995. For the text of the agreement, see UN Document S/1995/951, 15 November 1995 (Annex).

8 See 'Report of the Secretary-General Pursuant to Security Council Resolution 1025 (1995)', UN Document S/1995/1028, 13 December 1995, para. 14.

9 Tim Judah, *Kosovo: War and Revenge* (New Haven: Yale University Press, 2000).

10 For details of the post-war conditions, see 'Report of the Secretary-General on the United Nations Interim Administration Mission in Kosovo', UN Document S/1999/779, 12 July 1999.

11 UN Security Council Resolution 1244 (1999) was adopted on 10 June 1999.

12 Figures from Jarat Chopra, 'The UN's Kingdom of East Timor', *Survival*, vol. 42, no. 3, Autumn 2000, p. 27. See also 'Report of the Secretary-General on the Situation in East Timor', UN Document S/1999/1024, 4 October 1999.

13 UN Security Council Resolution 1272 (1999), established the mission.

14 For instance, UNTAET alone among these three missions has exercised effective treaty-making powers. See Jarat Chopra, 'Introductory Note to UNTAET Regulation 13', *International Legal Materials*, vol. 36, July 2000, p. 936.

15 *The General Framework Agreement for Peace in Bosnia and Herzegovina*, Annex 10, Article II.1(a)(b). The Agreement was initialled in Dayton on 21 November 1995 and signed in Paris on 14 December 1995.

16 The powers of the Brčko Supervisor are specified in the 'Arbitral Tribunal for Dispute over Inter-Entity Boundary in

Brcko Area Award' of 14 February 1997 and 'Final Award' of 5 March 1999, both available at http://www.ohr.int under 'Brcko Arbitration'.

17 Pjer Šimunović, 'A Framework for Success: Contextual Factors in the UNTAES Operation in Eastern Slavonia', *International Peacekeeping*, vol. 6, no. 1, Spring 1999, p. 131.

18 The relevant UN Security Council resolutions affirm the 'commitment of all Member States to the sovereignty and territorial integrity of the Federal Republic of Yugoslavia' or use similar language to that effect.

19 The launch of an armed Albanian insurgency in Western Macedonia in March 2001 provided evidence of the existence of this military infrastructure.

20 Department of Reconstruction (EU Pillar), United Nations Mission in Kosovo, *Kosovo 2001–2003: From Reconstruction to Growth*, Pristina, December 2000, p. 9.

21 Author interviews with World Bank officials. See also International Crisis Group, *Kosovo Report Card*, ICG Balkans Report No. 100 (Pristina/Brussels: ICG, 28 August 2000), pp. 35–8.

22 Chopra, 'The UN's Kingdom of East Timor', p. 28.

23 See Anthony Borden and Richard Caplan, 'The Former Yugoslavia: The War and the Peace Process' in *SIPRI Yearbook 1996* (Oxford: Oxford University Press for SIPRI, 1996), pp. 204–10.

24 See Elaine Scholino, Roger Cohen and Stephen Engelberg, 'Balkan Accord: The Play-by-Play', *New York Times*, 23 November 1995; and Richard Holbrooke, *To End a War* (New York: Random House, 1998).

25 *Constitution of Bosnia and Herzegovina*, Article I(3). The Constitution is Annex 4 of the Dayton agreement.

26 *Constitution of Bosnia and Herzegovina*, Article IV(3) and Article V(2).

27 Lenard J. Cohen, *Broken Bonds: Yugoslavia's Disintegration and Balkan Politics in Transition*, 2nd ed. (Boulder: Westview Press, 1995), chapters 6 and 7.

28 Roy Gutman, 'Signed, Sealed, Undelivered', *War Report*, no. 38, November/December 1995, pp. 3–8. See also Ivo H. Daalder, *Getting to Dayton: The Making of America's Bosnia Policy* (Washington, DC: Brookings Institution, 2000), pp. 117–27. Holbrooke (*To End a War*, pp. 166–7) claims to have urged the Bosnians and Croatians to continue the offensive and only to refrain from taking Banja Luka, which would have precipitated the mass flight of an estimated 100,000 Serbs.

29 Holbrooke, *To End a War*, pp. 166–7.

30 House of Commons, Foreign Affairs Committee, Session 1999–2000, Fourth Report, *Kosovo* (London: HMSO, 2000), vol. 1, para. 118.

31 Dietrich Rauschning, 'International Trusteeship System', in Bruno Simma (ed.), *The Charter of the United Nations: A Commentary* (Munich: C.H. Beck, 1995), pp. 938–9.

32 The Peace Implementation Council, made up of 55 governments and international organisations, was established by the Peace Implementation Conference on 8 and 9 December 1995. UN Security Council Resolution 1031 (15 December 1995) endorsed the establishment of the PIC. The PIC works through a Steering Board comprising representatives of Canada, France, Germany, Italy,

Japan, Russia, the United Kingdom, the United States, the Presidency of the European Union, the European Commission and the Organization of the Islamic Conference. See 'Conclusions of the Peace Implementation Conference held at Lancaster House', *International Legal Materials*, vol. 35 (1996), p. 223.

33 Marcus Cox, 'The Dayton Agreement in Bosnia and Herzegovina: A Study of Implementation Strategies', *British Yearbook of International Law*, vol. 70 (Oxford: Clarendon Press, 1999), p. 205. For details of the international deliberations over the role of the High Representative, see Carl Bildt, *Peace Journey: The Struggle for Peace in Bosnia* (London: Weidenfeld & Nicolson, 1998), chapter 9.

34 *The General Framework Agreement for Peace in Bosnia and Herzegovina*, Annex 10, Article II.1(c).

35 *Ibid.*

36 Author interviews with World Bank officials. See also Organisation for Economic Co-operation and Development, Development Assistance Committee, Informal Task Force on Conflict, Peace and Development Co-Operation, *The Limits and Scope for the Use of Development Assistance Incentives and Disincentives for Influencing Conflict Situations. Case Study: Bosnia and Herzegovina* (Paris: OECD, September 1999), p. 31.

37 European Stability Initiative, *Reshaping International Priorities in Bosnia and Herzegovina. Part II: International Power in Bosnia* (Berlin/Brussels/Sarajevo: ESI, 30 March 2000), p. 46. See also International Crisis Group, *Reunifying Mostar: Opportunities for Progress*, ICG Balkans Report No. 90 (Sarajevo/Washington/Brussels: ICG, 19 April 2000), p. 46.

38 Author interviews with UNHCR, OSCE and OHR officials in Bosnia.

39 Michael Steiner, ' "Don't Fool Around with Principles" ', *Transitions*, vol. 4, no. 3, August 1997, p. 39.

40 'Report of the Secretary-General on the United Nations Interim Administration Mission in Kosovo', UN Document S/1999/779, 12 July 1999, para. 44.

41 Author interviews with UNMIK officials.

42 Annex 10, Article II (9).

43 'Report of the Secretary-General Pursuant to Security Council Resolution 1025 (1995)', S/1995/1028, para. 13. See also UN Security Council Resolution 1037, 15 January 1996.

44 United Nations, Department of Peacekeeping Operations, Lessons Learned Unit, *The United Nations Transitional Administration in Eastern Slavonia, Baranja and Western Sirmium (UNTAES), January 1996–January 1998: Lessons Learned* (New York: UN Department of Public Information, 1998), para. 27.

45 *Ibid.*, paras 20–22.

46 Author interview with former UNTAES official.

47 Derek Boothby, 'Probing the Successful Application of Leverage in the UNTAES Operation', paper presented for a round-table meeting, 'Applying Leverage: Lessons from the United Nations Operations in Mozambique and Eastern Slavonia', New York University School of Law, New York, 8 October 1999, p. 7. Boothby is a former deputy transitional administrator of UNTAES (1996–7).

Chapter 2

1 'Report of the Panel on United Nations Peace Operations' (the Brahimi Report), UN Document A/55/505-S/2000/809, 21 August 2000, para. 87.

2 On the notion of spoilers and peace processes generally, see Stephen John Stedman, 'Spoiler Problems in Peace Processes', *International Security*, vol. 22, no. 2, Autumn 1997, pp. 5–53.

3 Michael J. Dziedzic and Andrew Bair, 'Bosnia and the International Police Task Force' in Robert B. Oakley, Michael J. Dziedzic and Eliot M. Goldberg (eds), *Policing the New World Disorder: Peace Operations and Public Security* (Washington, DC: National Defense University Press, 1998), pp. 253–314.

4 *Ibid.*, p. 310.

5 Only in Pristina and Prizren did UNMIK police have 'police primacy'. Assembly of the Western European Union, 'International Policing in South-Eastern Europe', Report of the Political Committee, Forty-Sixth Session, Document C/1721, 15 November 2000, para. 40.

6 'Report of the Secretary-General Pursuant to Resolution 1035 (1995)', UN Document S/1996/210, 29 March 1996, para. 6.

7 Author interviews with UNMIK officials in Pristina. The OSCE had begun planning for the establishment of an international police force that could take over from its Kosovo Verification Mission, but leading states appear to have concluded that it was too ambitious a task for the organisation. See Espen Barth Eide and Tor Tanke Holm, 'Postscript: Towards Executive Authority Policing? The Lessons of Kosovo', *International*

Peacekeeping, vol. 6, no. 4, Winter 1999, p. 215.

8 Chuck Call and Michael Barnett, 'Looking for a Few Good Cops: Peacekeeping, Peacebuilding and CIVPOL', *International Peacekeeping*, vol. 6, no. 4, Winter 1999, p. 51.

9 Author interviews with CIVPOL officials in Dili.

10 International Crisis Group, *Kosovo Report Card*, ICG Balkans Report No. 100 (Pristina/Brussels: ICG, 28 August 2000), p. 44.

11 'Report of the Secretary-General Pursuant to Resolution 1035 (1995)', UN Document S/1996/210, 29 March 1996, para. 3.

12 Assembly of the Western European Union, 'International Policing in South-Eastern Europe', para. 79, and 'Report of the Secretary-General on the United Nations Mission in Bosnia and Herzegovina', UN Document S/2000/1137, 30 November 2000, paras 10–12, 34.

13 Non-police tasks were estimated to be absorbing up to 20 percent of UNMIK's police resources in the early months of 2000. See 'Report of the Secretary-General on the United Nations Interim Administration Mission in Kosovo', UN Document S/2000/177, 3 March 2000, para. 41.

14 Author interviews with CIVPOL officers, Dili.

15 Jane M.O. Sharp, 'Dayton Report Card', *International Security*, vol. 22, no. 3, Winter 1996/97, p. 121.

16 Richard Holbrooke, *To End a War* (New York: Random House, 1998), pp. 218–23.

17 For details of the violence, see Human Rights Watch, *Federal Republic of Yugoslavia: Abuses Against Serbs and Roma in the New Kosovo* (New York: Human Rights Watch, August 1999).

18 David Rohde, ' "Serbian Zone" Decreed in Challenge to NATO', *International Herald Tribune*, 23 June 1999.

19 UNMIK Regulation No. 2000/6, promulgated on 15 March 2000, allows for international judges to select and take responsibility for cases, and for international prosecutors to perform their own investigations. UNMIK Regulation No. 2000/64, of 15 December 2000, allows for a local prosecutor, defence counsel or the accused to petition for assignment of an international judge or prosecutor where this is considered necessary to ensure the independence and impartiality of the judiciary or the proper administration of justice. UNTAET Regulation No. 2000/11, adopted on 6 March 2000, allows for the appointment of international judges alongside East Timorese judges to hear cases concerning serious criminal offences.

20 Author interviews with KFOR officials in Prizren. See also Lawyers Committee for Human Rights, *A Fragile Peace: Laying the Foundations for Justice in Kosovo* (New York: Lawyers Committee for Human Rights, October 1999), pp. 3–6.

21 Author interviews with CIVPOL officials in Kosovo and East Timor. See also 'Report of the Panel on United Nations Peace Operations', para. 83.

22 For details of the buy-back programme see Derek Boothby, *The UNTAES Experience: Weapons Buy-back in Eastern Slavonia, Baranja and Western Sirmium (Croatia)*, BICC Brief 12 (Bonn: Bonn International Center for Conversion, October 1998).

23 The 'Undertaking of Demilitarisation and Transformation of the KLA' concluded between the KLA and KFOR on 21 June 1999 established a 90-day period of demilitarisation during which the KLA surrendered some 10,000 weapons, 5.5 million rounds of ammunition and 27,000 grenades (*Kosovo Report Card*, p. 10). On 21 September 1999 the commander of KFOR, Lt Gen. Mike Jackson, declared that the KLA had complied with the terms of the KLA–KFOR agreement. See 'UN Signs Plans to Transform Kosovo Liberation Army into Civilian Corps', *Kosovo News Reports*, 21 September 1999, available at http://www.un.org/peace/kosovo/news/99/sep99_3.htm#Anchor70.

24 UNTAET Regulation No. 2001/1 (31 January 2001).

25 'East Timor – Reinsertion of Former Combatants', *IOM Briefing Notes*, 2 February 2001.

26 The arms-reduction measures are specified in Annex 1B (Agreement on Regional Stabilization) of the Dayton accord. On 'train and equip', see 'Concern Over Arms Delivery to Bosnia', *Financial Times*, 23 October 1996. The policy, insisted upon by the United States, was opposed by the Europeans, who considered it unwise to introduce more arms into the conflict zone.

27 For the difficulties associated with international efforts to achieve state-level defence institutions and policies, see under 'Military Issues' in 'Report of the High Representative for Implementation of the Peace Agreement to the Secretary-General of the United Nations', 17 October 2000 and 12 March 2001.

28 Amnesty International, *Bosnia-Herzegovina: The International Community's Responsibility to Ensure Human Rights* (London: Amnesty International, June 1996), p. 84.

[29] *The General Framework Agreement for Peace in Bosnia and Herzegovina,* Annex 7, Chapter One, Article I(1)(2).

[30] European Stability Initiative, *Reshaping International Priorities in Bosnia and Herzegovina. Part III: The End of the Nationalist Regimes and the Future of the Bosnian State* (Berlin/Brussels/Sarajevo: ESI, 22 March 2001), pp. 10–12.

[31] 'Refugees in Bosnia and Herzegovina: Prospects for Reintegration', *IISS Strategic Comments,* vol. 6, issue 8, October 2000. The task force was established at an informal meeting of international agencies in Geneva on 20 January 1997.

[32] *Ibid.* According to the OHR, roughly 67,000 minority returns were registered in 2000, compared with 41,000 in 1999. In reality the number of returns is greater, as not all returnees register (so that they may continue to draw benefits from the other entity). See 'Report by the High Representative for Implementation of the Peace Agreement to the Secretary-General of the United Nations', 12 March 2001, para. 35.

[33] In this regard see the interview with James Dobbin, US Assistant Secretary for European Affairs, 'Steady as She Goes', *NATO Review,* vol. 49, Spring 2001, pp. 9–11.

[34] 'Report by the High Representative for Implementation of the Peace Agreement to the Secretary-General of the United Nations', 10 December 1996, para. 51. See also International Crisis Group, *Bosnia's Refugee Logjam Breaks: Is the International Community Ready?* ICG Balkans Report No. 95 (Sarajevo/Washington/Brussels: ICG, 31 May 2000), pp. 14–15.

[35] Author interview with a former UNTAES official. For UN complaints about Zagreb's withholding of payment for public service (police) salaries, see 'Report of the Secretary-General on the United Nations Transitional Administration for Eastern Slavonia, Baranja and Western Sirmium', UN Document S/1996/883, 28 October 1996, para. 14.

[36] Cited in Jelena Smoljan, *Employment Policy within the Process of Peaceful Reintegration of Eastern Slavonia,* unpublished MPhil thesis in European Politics and Society, University of Oxford, 2002. The UN estimates that far fewer Serbs – 10 percent of a total population of 130,000 – emigrated in the course of the UNTAES mandate. See 'Report of the Secretary-General on the United Nations Transitional Administration for Eastern Slavonia, Baranja and Western Sirmium', UN Document S/1997/953, 4 December 1997, para. 6.

[37] 'Report by the High Representative for Implementation of the Peace Agreement to the Secretary-General of the United Nations', 1 November 1999, para. 124.

[38] In East Timor claims are being made even by exiles from the Portuguese colonial era. See Catherine Scott, *East Timor: Transition to Statehood* (London: Catholic Institute for International Relations, 2001), pp. 35–6. UNTAET has studiously avoided the question of property rights beyond registering them.

[39] 'Report by the High Representative for Implementation of the Peace Agreement to the Secretary-General of the United Nations', 17 October 2000, para. 46.

[40] 'Report by the High Representative for Implementation

of the Peace Agreement to the Secretary-General of the United Nations', 12 March 2001, para. 38.

[41] Author interviews with OHR officials, Sarajevo.

[42] For other earlier experiments in international civil administration, see Jarat Chopra, *Peace-Maintenance: The Evolution of International Political Authority* (London: Routledge, 1999), chapter 3.

[43] 'Report of the High Representative for Implementation of the Peace Agreement to the Secretary-General of the United Nations', 14 July 1998, para. 80.

[44] For a discussion of the effectiveness of these institutions, see European Stability Initiative, *Reshaping International Priorities in Bosnia and Herzegovina. Part II: International Power in Bosnia*, (Berlin/Brussels/Sarajevo: ESI, 30 March 2000). On the IMC, see Katrin Metcalf Nyman and Krister Thelin, 'Media and the Rule of Law: Regulation for the Peace Process in Bosnia and Herzegovina', *Särtryck ur Juridisk Tidskrift*, no. 3 (1999–2000), pp. 579–90.

[45] UNMIK Regulation No. 2000/1, 'On the Kosovo Joint Interim Administrative Structure', 14 January 2001, Sections 4–6.

[46] *Ibid.*, Section 7.

[47] Author interviews with UNMIK officials.

[48] Only the deadline for elections is specified in the Dayton accord. See *The General Framework Agreement for Peace in Bosnia and Herzegovina*, Annex 3, Article II.4.

[49] Patrick Moore, 'A Royal Mess', *Transition*, 18 October 1996, p. 77.

[50] Eligible citizens were expected to vote in the municipality where they resided in 1991 but could apply to the Provisional Election Commission to vote elsewhere. See *The General Framework Agreement for Peace in Bosnia and Herzegovina*, Annex 3, Article IV.

[51] Indicted or convicted war criminals, however, were barred from standing for or holding public office. See *Constitution of Bosnia and Herzegovina*, Article IX.

[52] Hobrooke cited in Fareed Zakaria, 'The Rise of Illiberal Democracy', *Foreign Affairs*, vol. 76, no. 6, November/December 1997, p. 22.

[53] Author interviews with local political leaders in Dili and the districts. See also 'It's Worrying, This Democracy', *The Economist*, 28 June 2001, p. 64.

[54] The UN established the Kosovo Transitional Council, consisting of six members of the Albanian community, two Serbs, one Muslim and one Turk, on 16 July 1999. UNMIK Regulation 2000/1 (14 January 2000) expanded the KTC to 36 members. UNTAET Regulation 1999/2 (2 December 1999) established the 15-member National Consultative Council.

[55] World Bank, 'Trust Fund for East Timor', Update No. 2, 6 September 2000, pp. 1–2. The UN administration has been lukewarm in its support of the CEP. See Jarat Chopra, 'The UN's Kingdom of East Timor', *Survival*, vol. 42, no. 3, Autumn 2000, pp. 27–39.

[56] As one senior UNTAET official confirmed to the author.

[57] UNTAET Regulation No. 2000/24 and UNTAET Regulation No. 2000/23 respectively.

[58] East Timorese were initially given four portfolios out of eight (internal administration, infrastructure, economic affairs and social affairs), and later five out of nine (foreign affairs was the fifth). See 'Report of the Secretary-General on the United Nations Transitional Administration in East Timor (for the period 27 July 2000 to 16

January 2001)', UN Document S/2001/42, 16 January 2001, para. 9. Since 20 September 2001, all eleven UNTAET ministers have been East Timorese.

[59] Strictly speaking the PIC did not confer new powers on the High Representative but rather endorsed his 'interpretation' of his authority deriving from the Dayton accord. See *Bosnia and Herzegovina 1998: Self-Sustaining Structures*, Bonn Peace Implementation Conference, 10 December 1997, Annex, Article XI (2) in *Bosnia and Herzegovina: Essential Texts*, 2nd ed. (Sarajevo: Office of the High Representative: January 1998), pp. 202–3.

[60] Information compiled from various sources, including reports of the High Representative to the UN Secretary-General.

[61] See, for instance, David Chandler, *Bosnia: Faking Democracy after Dayton* (London: Pluto Press, 1999).

[62] International Crisis Group, *Why Will No One Invest in Bosnia and Herzegovina?* ICG Report No. 64 (Sarajevo: ICG, 21 April 1999).

[63] European Bank for Reconstruction and Development, *Bosnia and Herzegovina: Investment Profile 2001* (London: EBRD, 2001), p. 9.

[64] USAID, 'Payment Bureaus in Bosnia and Herzegovina: Obstacles to Development and a Strategy for Orderly Transformation' (Sarajevo: USAID, 1999) cited in International Crisis Group, *Why Will No One Invest in Bosnia and Herzegovina?*, p. 6 (fn. 17).

[65] Frances Stewart and Valpy FitzGerald, 'Introduction: Assessing the Economic Costs of War' in Frances Stewart and Valpy FitzGerald (eds), *War and Underdevelopment* (Oxford: Oxford University Press, 2001), vol. 1.

[66] Stability Pact for South East Europe, *Cologne Document*, Cologne, 10 June 1999, available at http://www.stabilitypact.org/stabilitypactcgi/catalog/cat_descr.cgi?prod_id = 409. Working Table II is concerned specifically with economic reconstruction.

[67] International Crisis Group, *After Milosevic: A Practical Agenda for Lasting Balkans Peace*, ICG Balkans Report No. 108 (Brussels: ICG, 1 April 2001), pp. 239–48.

[68] United Nations Economic Commission for Europe, *Economic Survey of Europe 2000*, No. 1 (Geneva: United Nations, 2000), pp. 7–8.

[69] For a discussion of 'peace conditionality', see James K. Boyce and Manual Pastor, Jr., 'Aid for Peace: Can International Financial Institutions Help Prevent Conflict?', *World Policy Journal*, vol. 15, no. 2, Summer 1998, pp. 42–9. For a discussion of this issue in the Bosnian context, see Carl Bildt, *Peace Journey: The Struggle for Peace in Bosnia* (London: Weidenfeld & Nicolson, 1998), chapter 13.

Chapter 3

[1] A notable exception is the United Nations Transitional Assistance Group (UNTAG), which oversaw Namibia's transition to independence. UNTAG was established in 1978 but did not begin operations until 1989, because of South Africa's refusal to allow the mission to deploy. The long delay gave the UN more time to plan the mission than is usually the case. See Simon Chesterman, *East Timor in Transition: From Conflict Prevention to State-Building* (New York: International Peace Academy, 2001), p. 7.

[2] Author interviews with UNTAET officials, Dili.

[3] 'Question of East Timor: Report of the Secretary-General', UN Document S/1999/862, 9 August 1999, para. 12.

[4] 'Report of the Panel on United Nations Peace Operations', para. 200.

[5] Jarat Chopra, 'The UN's Kingdom of East Timor', *Survival*, vol. 42, no. 3, Autumn 2000, p. 32; letter from Chopra to Vieira de Mello, 17 November 1999; author interviews with UNTAET officials, Dili.

[6] Author interview with UNTAET official, Dili.

[7] Sergio Vieira de Mello, 'How Not to Run a Country: Lessons for the UN from Kosovo and East Timor', unpublished manuscript.

[8] Author interview, Pristina.

[9] Author interviews with UNMIK officials, Pristina.

[10] The PIC agendas are available at the OHR website: http://www.ohr.int, under 'Peace Implementation Council'.

[11] And yet, with respect to NATO's entry into Kosovo, the Defence Committee of the UK House of Commons observed in a recent inquiry, 'it is a matter of concern that, after months of waiting for air strikes to force Milosevic into an agreement, when the time came, NATO was still scrambling to gather the requisite number of troops together for its peace implementation force'. House of Commons, Defence Committee, Session 1999–2000, Fourteenth Report, *Lessons of Kosovo* (London: HMSO, 2000), vol. 1, para. 282.

[12] 'Report of the Panel on United Nations Peace Operations', para. 183.

[13] Shepard Forman, Stewart Patrick and Dirk Salomons, *Recovering from Conflict: Strategy for An International Response* (New York: Center on International Cooperation, 2000), pp. 17–18.

[14] Author interviews with UNTAET officials, Dili.

[15] Indeed, East Timor's troubles after 1975 are in part the legacy of Portugal's sudden withdrawal and its failure to prepare the ground more carefully for a transfer of power. See Peter Carey and G. Carter Bentley, *East Timor at the Crossroads: The Forging of a Nation* (London and New York: Social Science Research Council and Cassell, 1995).

[16] *The General Framework Agreement for Peace in Bosnia and Herzegovina*, Annex 10. See also 'Conclusions of the Peace Implementation Conference Held at Lancaster House', London 8–9 December 1995, in *Bosnia and Herzegovina: Essential Texts*, 2nd ed. (Sarajevo: Office of the High Representative: January 1998), p. 58.

[17] UNTAET Regulation No. 2000/24 (14 July 2000), Section 10.

[18] 'Declaration of the Peace Implementation Council', 23–4 May 2000, Brussels, available at http://www.ohr.int/docu/p200005 24a.htm.

[19] Decision available at http://www.ohr.int/decisions/200 01112b.htm.

[20] *Constitution of Bosnia and Herzegovina*, Article III (3)(a).

[21] *Constitution of the Republika Srpska*, Article 68.

[22] Author interviews with UNTAET officials, Dili and London. See also Chopra, 'The UN's Kingdom of East Timor', pp. 33–4; and Chesterman, *East Timor in Transition*, pp. 13–14.

[23] Transcript of the address of SRSG Sergio Vieira de Mello at the first CNRT Congress, *UNTAET Daily Briefing*, 21 August 2000, available at http://www.un.org/peace/etimor/DB/DB210800.HTM.

[24] *Office of the High Representative Bulletin*, No. 54, 15 July 1997,

available at http://www.ohr.int/
bulletins/b970715.htm#2;
European Stability Initiative,
*Reshaping International Priorities in
Bosnia and Herzegovina. Part II:
International Power in Bosnia,*
(Berlin/Brussels/Sarajevo: ESI, 30
March 2000), pp. 35–6.

25 OSCE, Provisional Election
Commission, *Bilten,* No. 3
(October 1996), p. 119, cited in
David Chandler, *Bosnia: Faking
Democracy After Dayton* (London:
Pluto Press, 1999), p. 122.

26 Ted Galen Carpenter, 'Bringing
PC "Democracy" Back to Bosnia',
Washington Times, 24 October
1997, cited in Chandler, *Bosnia:
Faking Democracy After Dayton,*
p. 158.

27 International Crisis Group,
*Bosnia's November Elections: Dayton
Stumbles,* ICG Balkans Report No.
104 (Sarajevo/Brussels: ICG, 18
December 2000).

28 International Crisis Group, *State of
the Balkans,* ICG Balkans Report
No. 47 (Brussels: ICG, 4
November 1998), p. 13.

29 United Nations, *Agenda for
Democratization: Supplement to
Reports A/50/332 and A/51/512 on
Democratization,* UN Document
A/51/761, 20 December 1996,
paras 10 and 21.

30 Joel Blocker, 'Romania/Hungary:
Historic Basic Treaty Signed
Today', *RFE/RL Weekday Magazine,*
16 September 1996, online edition
at http://www.rferl.org.

31 East Timor stands to reap
hundreds of millions of dollars in
royalties from the Timor Gap
treaty that the UN initialled with
Australia on 5 July 2001. For
treaty provisions see 'Summary of
Timor Sea Arrangement',
UNTAET Press Office, Dili, 5 July
2001. For discussion of the
relationship between economic
prosperity and democracy, see
Seymour Martin Lipset, 'The

Social Requisites of Democracy
Revisited: 1993 Presidential
Address', *American Sociological
Review,* vol. 59, no. 1, February
1994, pp. 1–22.

32 This argument is articulated in
European Stability Initiative,
*Reshaping International Priorities in
Bosnia and Herzegovina. Part III:
The End of the Nationalist Regimes
and the Future of the Bosnian State*
(Berlin/Brussels/Sarajevo: ESI, 22
March 2001).

33 Dietrich Rauschning,
'International Trusteeship System',
in Bruno Simma (ed.), *The Charter
of the United Nations: A
Commentary* (Munich: C.H. Beck,
1995), pp. 933–4.

34 The Peace Implementation
Conference, meeting in London
on 8–9 December 1995, designated
Carl Bildt as the first High
Representative. The UN Security
Council in turn endorsed the
establishment of a High
Representative and agreed the
appointment of Bildt (UNSC
Resolution 1031, 15 December
1995).

35 The World Bank Inspection Panel,
established in 1993, is a
three-member body that hears
complaints from private
individuals who believe that they
have been, or are likely to be,
adversely affected by the Bank's
own policies. See Ibrahim F. I.
Shihata, *The World Bank Inspection
Panel: In Practice* (New York:
World Bank/Oxford University
Press, 2000).

36 UNMIK Regulation No. 2000/38,
30 June 2000. UNTAET created
the Office of the Ombudsperson
without, however, adopting a
regulation establishing it.

37 Ombudsperson Institution in
Kosovo, Special Report No.1 on
the Compatibility with
Recognized International
Standards of UNMIK Regulation

No. 2000/47 on the Status, Privileges and Immunities of KFOR and UNMIK and Their Personnel in Kosovo (18 August 2000) and on The Implementation of the Above Regulation, cited in Amnesty International, *East Timor: Justice Past, Present and Future*, AI Index ASA 57/001/2001, 27 July 2001, available at http://web. amnesty.org/ai.nsf/print/ASA5700 12001?OpenDocument.

38 UNTAET Regulation No. 2000/23 (14 July 2000) and UNTAET Regulation No. 2000/24 (14 July 2000).

39 'Cabinet Approves Regulations on Defence Force and the Registration of Political Parties', *UNTAET Daily Press Briefing*, 17 January 2001, available at http://www.un.org/peace/ etimor/DB/Db170101.htm.

40 International Crisis Group, *Aid and Accountability: Dayton Implementation*, ICG Bosnia Report No. 17 (Sarajevo: ICG, 24 November 1996), p. 16.

41 Ngaire Woods and Amrita Narlikar, 'Governance and the Limits of Accountability: The WTO, the IMF and the World Bank', *International Social Science Journal*, vol. 53, no. 170, December 2001, pp. 569–83.

42 See Anthony Adair, 'A Code of Conduct for NGOs – A Necessary Reform', an Institute of Economic Affairs Website Discussion Paper, April 1999, available at http://www.iea.org.uk/wpapers/ NGO.htm.

43 For a comparative assessment of evaluative reports – both NGO and official – of the humanitarian response to the 1999 Kosovo crisis, see Active Learning Network for Accountability and Performance in Humanitarian Action, *Humanitarian Action: Learning from Evaluation* (London: Overseas Development Institute, 2001).

44 Author interview with UNTAET official, Dili.

45 Mats R. Berdal, *Whither UN Peacekeeping?* Adelphi Paper 281 (Oxford University Press for the IISS, 1993), p. 13. The single-minded focus on elections in Cambodia was the result more of necessity than design. See Janet E. Heininger, *Peacekeeping in Transition: The United Nations in Cambodia* (New York: Twentieth Century Fund Press, 1994), p. 38.

46 Samuel H. Barnes, 'The Contribution of Democracy to Rebuilding Postconflict Societies', *American Journal of International Law*, vol. 95, no. 1, January 2001, p. 95.

47 United Nations, Department of Peacekeeping Operations, Lessons Learned Unit, *The United Nations Transitional Administration in Eastern Slavonia, Baranja and Western Sirmium (UNTAES), January 1996–January 1998: Lessons Learned* (New York: UN Department of Public Information, 1998), p. 34; 'Report of the Secretary-General on the Situation in Croatia', UN Document S/1997/487, 23 June 1997, para. 3.

48 'Kosovo: Security Council, Annan Welcome "Orderly and Peaceful" Assembly Elections', *Kosovo News Reports*, 20 November 2001, available at http://www.un.org/ peace/kosovo/news/kosovo2.htm# Anchor40.

49 UNMIK Regulation No. 2001/9.

50 These are: the Roma, Askhali and Egyptian communities (4 seats); the Bosniac community (3 seats), the Turkish community (2 seats) and the Gorani community (1 seat). *Constitutional Framework*, Chapter 9.1.3.

51 *Constitutional Framework*, Chapter 9.1.39–42. Unlike in Bosnia, the matter can be decided expeditiously by a three-member

panel made up of representatives of the two sides and one member designated by the Transitional Administrator, taking its decisions by a majority of its members.

52 *Constitutional Framework*, Chapter 4.

53 For details see Sally Morphet, 'Current Civil Administration: The Need for Political Legitimacy', *International Peacekeeping*, forthcoming 2002.

54 'Report of the Secretary-General on the Situation in Croatia', UN Document S/1997/487, 23 June 1997, para. 48.

55 Agreements listed in 'Report of the Secretary-General on the United Nations Transitional Administration for Eastern Slavonia, Baranja and Western Sirmium', UN Document S/1997/953, 4 December 1997, Annex I.

56 OSCE Mission to the Republic of Croatia, 'Report of the OSCE Mission to the Republic of Croatia on Croatia's Progress in Meeting International Commitments Since November 2000', SEC.FR/156/01, 14 March 2001.

57 The UN Secretariat is more willing now to contemplate withdrawal in cases where 'the mission is not making a positive contribution and there are no apparent prospects for its doing so'. See 'No Exit Without Strategy: Security Council Decision-making and the Closure or Transition of United Nations Peacekeeping Operations', UN Document S/2001/394, 20 April 2001, para. 26.

Chapter 4

1 'Report of the Panel on United Nations Peace Operations', UN Document A/55/505-S/2000/809, 21 August 2000.

2 *Ibid.*, paras 76–83.

3 *Ibid.*, para. 172.

4 UN General Assembly Resolution A/Res/55/238, adopted on 23 December 2000.

5 'Implementation of the Report of the Panel on United Nations Peace Operations: Report of the Advisory Committee on Administrative and Budgetary Questions', UN Document A/56/478, 16 October 2001, para. 99.

6 The Independent Inquiry into Rwanda cited the lack of contingency planning as one of the factors that contributed to the UN's failure to prevent genocide there. It recommended '[i]ncreasing preparedness to conduct contingency planning, both for expected new peacekeeping operations and to meet possible needs to adjust mandates of existing operations'. See 'Report of the Independent Inquiry into the Actions of the United Nations during the 1994 Genocide in Rwanda', 15 December 1999, available at http://www.un.org/News/ossg/rwanda_report.htm.

7 For a discussion of the institutional framework for European Security and Defence Policy, see Jolyon Howorth, *European Integration and Defence: The Ultimate Challenge?* Chaillot Paper 43 (Paris: Western European Union Institute for Security Studies, November 2000), pp. 32–7.

8 'Declaration on the Establishment of a Policy Planning and Early Warning Unit', *Treaty of Amsterdam*, Declaration No. 6, 2 October 1997.

9 'Presidency Report', Nice European Council Meeting, 7–9 December 2000, Annex V. The EUMS was established on 22 January 2001 with Council Decision 2001/80/CFSP.

10 The Petersberg tasks were agreed at a ministerial meeting of the Western European Union in Petersberg, near Bonn on 19 June 1992.

11 'Implementation of the Recommendations of the Special Committee on Peacekeeping Operations and the Panel on United Nations Peace Operations: Report of the Secretary-General', paras 234–8.

12 'Report of the Secretary-General on the Implementation of the Report of the Panel on United Nations Peace Operations', UN Document A/55/502, 20 October 2000, paras 49–66.

13 *Ibid.*, para. 53.

14 'Report of the Secretary-General: Implementation of the Recommendations of the Special Committee on Peacekeeping Operations and the Panel on United Nations Peace Operations', paras 88–9; author interviews with UN officials, New York.

15 Author interviews with UN field personnel in UNTAES, UNMIK and UNTAET.

16 'Report of the Secretary-General: Implementation of the Recommendations of the Special Committee on Peacekeeping Operations and the Panel on United Nations Peace Operations', paras 66–7.

17 On the inadequacy of detention facilities, see 'Report of the Secretary-General on the United Nations Interim Administration Mission in Kosovo', UN Document S/2000/177, 3 March 2000, para. 114.

18 'Report of the Secretary-General: Implementation of the Recommendations of the Special Committee on Peacekeeping Operations and the Panel on United Nations Peace Operations', paras 128–9.

19 'Report of the Panel on United Nations Peace Operations', para. 88.

20 *Ibid.*, paras 118–26.

21 'Report of the Secretary-General: Implementation of the Recommendations of the Special Committee on Peacekeeping Operations and the Panel on United Nations Peace Operations', para. 132.

22 'Report of the Secretary-General on the Implementation of the Report of the Panel on United Nations Peace Operations', para. 95.

23 'Report of the Panel on United Nations Peace Operations', para. 123.

24 Author interview with Foreign and Commonwealth Office official, London.

25 'Presidency Conclusions', Santa Maria da Feira European Council Meeting, 19–20 June 2000, Appendix 4.

26 'EU Member States Police Capabilities for International Crisis Management', speech by Javier Solana to the EU Conference of National Police Commissioners, Brussels, 10 May 2001, Council of the European Union Press Release: Brussels (10–05–2001) – No. 0084/00.

27 See Office of International Information Programs, US Department of State, 'Summary of Presidential Decision Directive 71', 24 February 2000, available at http://www.fas.org/irp/offdocs/pdd/pdd-71-1.htm. As of October 2001, nearly 850 US police officers were serving in international peace operations, making the United States the largest police contributor.

28 'Misconduct, Corruption by US Police Mar Bosnia Mission', *Washington Post*, 29 May 2001.

29 Lucius Clay, *Decision in Germany* (London: William Heineman, 1950), p. 65.

30 Office of International Information Programs, US Department of State, 'White Paper: The Clinton Administration's Policy on Strengthening Criminal Justice Systems in Support of Peace Operations', 24 February 2000, available at http://www.fas.org/irp/offdocs/pdd/pdd-71–4.htm.

31 Sergio Vieira de Mello, 'How Not to Run a Country: Lessons for the UN from Kosovo and East Timor', unpublished manuscript.

32 'Report of the Panel on United Nations Peace Operations', para. 153.

33 'Report of the Secretary-General: Implementation of the Recommendations of the Special Committee on Peacekeeping Operations and the Panel on United Nations Peace Operations', para. 150.

34 Author interview with senior UNTAET official, Dili.

35 'Implementation of the Recommendations of the Special Committee on Peacekeeping Operations and the Panel on United Nations Peace Operations', para. 118; and 'UNMEE Military Observer Teams Complete Initial Deployment', UN Document UNMEE/PR/3, 25 September 2000.

36 'Report of the Panel on United Nations Peace Operations', para. 130.

37 'Report of the Office of Internal Oversight Services on the Audit of the Policies and Procedures of the Department of Peacekeeping Operations for Recruiting International Civilian Staff for Field Missions', UN Document A/56/202, 20 July 2001, paras 11–14.

38 Author interviews with East Timorese local leadership, Dili.

39 Author interview with senior UNTAET official, Dili.

40 Simon Chesterman, *Kosovo in Limbo: State-Building and 'Substantial Autonomy'* (New York: International Peace Academy, August 2001), p. 4.

41 For discussion of the UN's democratic deficit and proposals to remedy it, see Michael Renner, *Critical Juncture: The Future of Peacekeeping*, Worldwatch Paper 114 (Washington DC: Worldwatch Institute, 1993), pp. 54–8; and Vicenç Fisas, *Blue Geopolitics: The United Nations Reform and the Future of the Blue Helmets* (London: Pluto Press, 1995), chapters 1 and 2.

42 See 'Report of the Secretary-General on the United Nations Interim Administration Mission in Kosovo', UN Document S/1999/779, 12 July 1999, para. 110.

43 Author interviews with international and local officials and NGO representatives, East Timor.

44 Author interviews with UNMIK officials. Rugova can be said to be more moderate only because of his rejection of violence. He shares the same goals as Thaci.

45 Samuel H. Barnes, 'The Contribution of Democracy to Rebuilding Postconflict Societies', *American Journal of International Law*, vol. 95, no. 1, January 2001, pp. 86–101.

46 For the role and functions of the 'classical' ombudsman, see Donald C. Rowat, *The Ombudsman: Citizens' Defender*, 2nd ed. (London: George Allen & Unwin, 1968).

47 *Constitution of Bosnia and Herzegovina*, Article VI.

48 'Constitution Watch: Bosnia and Herzegovina', *East European Constitutional Review*, vol. 10, no. 1, Winter 2001, available at http://www.law.nyu.edu/eecr/vol10num1/constitutionwatch/bosnia.html.

10

Cambridge University Press,
2000), introduction.

2 Wolfgang Petritsch, 'Bosnien und
Herzegowina fünf Jahre nach
Dayton', *Südosteuropa Mitteilungen*,
vol. 40, no. 4 (2000), pp. 297–312.

3 On 'opportunistic interventions'
by regional powers, see Michael
E. Brown, 'The Causes and
Reg
Cor
(ed
of I

MA: MIT Press for the Center for
Science and International Affairs,
1996), chapter 17.

Jin Song, 'The Political Dynamics
of the Peacemaking Process in
Cambodia' in Michael W. Doyle *et
al.* (eds), *Keeping the Peace:
Multidimensional UN Operations in
Cambodia and El Salvador*
(Cambridge: Cambridge
University Press, 1997), pp. 53–81.

5 Robert Cooper, *The Post-modern
State and World Order*, 2nd ed.
(London: Demos and The Foreign
), p. 11.
Need for a
Financial Times,

DATE DUE

GAYLORD | | PRINTED IN U.S.A.